INNOVATION AND RECENT ADVANCEMENT
IN
FASHION AND TEXTILE

INNOVATION AND RECENT ADVANCEMENT IN **FASHION AND TEXTILE**

Dr. Reema Varshney
Ms. Nimisha Rana Chaudhary

HOW ACADEMICS
an imprint of Highlyy Publishing LLP

ISBN: 978-93-95522-15-1 (Hardback)
First Published : 2023

Published by : HOW ACADEMICS
an imprint of Highlyy Publishing LLP

Correspondence Address : 4/30 A II Floor, Double Storey Buildings
Vijay Nagar, Delhi-110009
Editorial: +91 9811026449
Sales : +91 9999953412
Email: info@howacademics.com
Website: www.howacademics.com

Printed in India

Preface

The clothing industry utilizes 93,000 billion cubic metres of water annually, enough for 5 million people's survival. It also accounts for 20 percent of the total water wasted worldwide. Producing clothing and footwear leads to 8 percent of GHGs (greenhouse gases). Each second, a quantity of textiles equal to a garbage truck is burned or buried. Undoubtedly, the era of fast fashion has led to an accelerated rise in these negative outcomes. Against this backdrop, the WWF issued clarion call years earlier for a shift towards slow fashion or a sustainable clothing and textile industry. Hence, bring equilibrium between fashion, textiles and environment an eco-friendly sustainable alternative is the only solutions. New innovations lead better solutions so that society as a whole will be benefitted.

This book comprises well-written review papers contributed by the experts in the field of Fashion and Textiles. Each review summarizes cutting edge researches on a specific approach in recent advancement in Fashion and Textiles. Many of these reviews are focused on the emerging topics like Technical Textiles, Microencapsulation finishing in textiles, naturally colored cotton, Protective Clothing and many more new emerging topics which contribute to the advancement of above fields.

We are grateful to all the contributors for their willingness to write paper on important aspects of advancements and innovation in the field of Fashion and Textile as well as submitting their chapters in a timely manner. We are grateful to the team of AICTE especially Mrs. Mamta Rani Aggarwal, Advisor, ATAL for motivating and conducting a research for sustainable fashion. We are thankful to Ms. Bela Gupta, Professor, Pearl Academy for her unconditional support for the book. We are also grateful to the Publishing House i.e. HOW Academics and their team especially Mr. Kanav Kansra for their untiring efforts to make this assignment a success.

Dr. Reema Varshney

Professor & Director, Vidya Institute of Fashion Technology, Meerut

Ms. Nimisha Rana Chaudhary

Assistant Professor, Vidya Institute of Fashion Technology, Meerut

Foreword

It is with great pleasure that I introduce the book 'Recent Advancements in Fashion and Textiles' to you. Dear reader, this book is a comprehensive compilation of thirteen research articles edited by the esteemed Professor, Dr. Reema Varshney and Assistant Professor, Ms. Nimisha Rana Chaurdhary. The book delves into the fascinating world of technical textiles, their applications in various industries, and the latest advancements in the field.

As we move towards a more technology-driven world, the textile industry has also been impacted significantly. With innovations in materials, techniques, and processes, the possibilities of what textiles can achieve are endless. Dr. Varshney, through carefully selected articles has beautifully captured the essence of this dynamic industry and its potential to transform our lives.

The book covers a wide range of topics, from the history and use of natural dyes to the use of artificial intelligence in textile design. It also highlights the importance of sustainable fashion and the need to move towards ethical and environmentally friendly practices in the industry. The articles are well-researched and provide valuable insights into the field of technical textiles.

One of the papers also highlights the need for protective clothing to ensure the well-being of workers who may be exposed to occupational or health hazards in different fields. The author draws attention to the ancestral craft of Pattu weaving and its importance in western Rajasthan.

As an educationist, I have understood and analyzed various complex, academic concepts, and ideas. However, reading this book has given me a new found appreciation for the intricacies and nuances of textile science and engineering. I am confident that this book will be a valuable resource for researchers, students, and professionals in the field of textiles and fashion.

I would like to extend my heartfelt congratulations to Dr. Reema Varshney on this impressive work. It is a testament to her knowledge, expertise, and dedication to the field. I am honoured to have had the opportunity to read and write the

'Foreword' of this book. I am sure that this book will be a valuable addition to any library.

So, without further ado, I invite you to turn the page and begin your reading journey into this remarkable book. May it inform, inspire, and challenge you in equal measure.

Sincerely,

Dr. Mamta Rani Agarwal
Advisor-I
AICTE Training and Learning, (ATAL), Academy, HQ
All India Council for Technical Education

Contents

1. Technical Textiles: The Future of Textiles

Dr. Deepti Bhargava, Assistant Professor

College of Community Science, Banda University of Agriculture and Technology, Banda, Uttar Pradesh

Abstract

Technical textiles are considered an amazing field in the range of textile science and engineering, which have diverse applications in all science and engineering sectors. The modern age is led by the versatile products of technical textiles. The technical textile can be defined, according to the Textile Terms & Definitions, published by the Textile Institute as, "textile materials and products manufactured primarily for their technical and performance properties rather than their aesthetic or decorative characteristics." Technical textile materials are designed to have high levels of physical, mechanical, thermal, and/or chemical properties for use in specific applications within industrial sectors such as earthworks, construction, civil engineering, transport, defence, medical, and healthcare. Sometimes other terms like industrial textiles, functional textiles, engineered textiles, performance textiles, etc. can be used instead of technical textiles.

Keywords: technical textile, functional textile, engineered textile, performance textile

Introduction

The definition of technical textiles adopted by the authoritative Textile Terms and Definitions, published by the Textile Institute, is 'textile materials and products manufactured primarily for their technical and performance properties rather than their aesthetic or decorative characteristics. For many years, the term 'industrial textiles' was widely used to encompass all textile products other than those intended for apparel, household, and furnishing end-uses. This is one of the most promising and faster-growing areas for the global and Indian textile industry indispensable part of human life encompasses an immense range and diversity of raw materials, processes, products, and applications that account for over one-quarter of all textile consumption in weight terms plays a crucial role in the Indian economy and infrastructural development. This usage has seemed increasingly inappropriate in the face of developing applications of textiles for medical, hygiene, sporting, transportation, construction, agricultural, and many other clearly non-industrial purposes. Industrial textiles are now more often viewed as a subgroup of a wider category of technical textiles, referring specifically to those textile products used in the course of manufacturing operations (such as filters, machine clothing, conveyor belts, abrasive substrates, etc.) or which are incorporated into other industrial products (such as electrical components and cables, flexible seals and diaphragms, or acoustic and thermal insulation for domestic and industrial appliances). The distinctiveness and confrontation of technical textiles lie in the need to support and apply the principles of textile science and technology to give solutions, mainly to technological problems but also often to engineering problems (Chaudhary and Shahid 2013.). It is expected that technical textiles would be one of the most promising sectors in this growth and the factors like, global economic change, strong government support, the introduction of appropriate legislation, the development of tests and standards, and widespread recognition of the need for more trained personnel, etc. also playing the valuable role in driving the industry to the farthest destination (Patel, 2010).

Classification of Technical Textiles and Their Applications:

International trade exhibition for technical textiles, Techtextil (organized biennially since the late 1980s by Messe Frankfurt in Germany and also in Osaka, Japan), defines 12 main application areas (of which textiles for industrial applications represent only one group):

- Agrotech: agriculture, aquaculture, horticulture, and forestry
- Buildtech: building and construction
- Clothtech: technical components of footwear and clothing
- Geotech: geotextiles and civil engineering
- Hometech: technical components of furniture, household textiles and floorcoverings
- Indutech: filtration, conveying, cleaning and other industrial uses
- Medtech: hygiene and medical
- Mobiltech: automobiles, shipping, railways and aerospace
- Oekotech: environmental protection
- Packtech: packaging
- Protech: personal and property protection
- Sporttech: sport and leisure

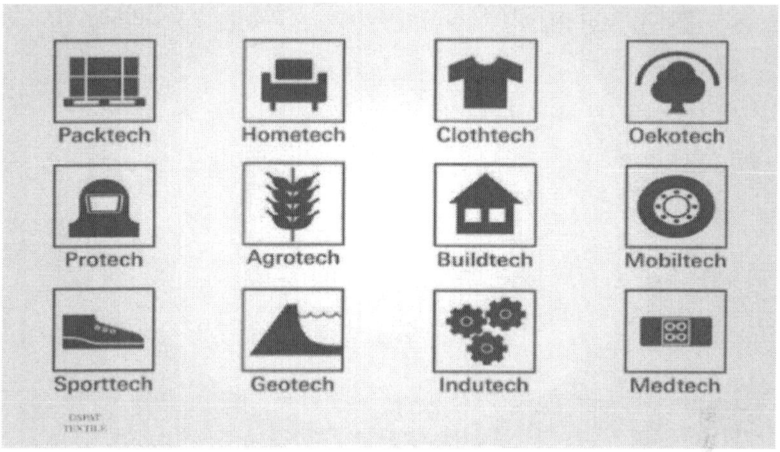

Fig.1.1 Applications of Technical Textiles

Above types of technical textiles are briefly described below:

1. Agrotech or Agro textiles:

The textiles used in agriculture are called as agro textiles. It deals with the technical textile products used in the agriculture, horticulture, forestry, farming and fishing industries. Depending upon the applications, the raw materials for aggrotech products must have these properties.

- Resistance to sunlight and weather (frost, wind, rain, hail storm, etc.)
- Resistance to microorganisms
- Long service life and lightweight
- Biodegradability
- Strength
- Elongation
- Stiffness
- Resistance to toxic environment

Both natural and synthetic fibers are used for aggrotech products. Some of the commonly used natural fibers for aggrotech products are jute, flax, ramie, etc. These fibers are used for their biodegradable property. Similarly, polypropylene (PP), polyethylene, nylon, and polyester, are also used for their good ultraviolet (UV) resistance, good strength and long service life properties. Weaving, knitting and non-woven technologies are used to manufacture aggrotech products. Some of the examples of aggrotech products are sunscreens, bird protection nets, plant nets, harvesting nets and packing material for agriculture products (Anonymous1. 2022).

Applications of Agro Textiles are:

1. Crop protection cover
2. Capillary matting
3. Land netting
4. Fishing ropes
5. Fishing nets
6. Anti-hail nets
7. Bird protection nets
8. Composite reinforcements
9. Protective clothing for employees
10. Transport textiles for tractors and lorries
11. Silos, tanks and piping etc.

Fig.1.2 Shade Net

Fig.1.3 Bird Protection Net

Fig.1.4 Mulch Mat

2. Buildtech or Building Textiles:

The textiles used in the construction and architectural application are called buildtech. This sector consists of technical textiles that are used in the construction of temporary buildings, permanent buildings and structures. These are widely used for roofing, insulation and cladding, acoustic and structural purposes. A major growth in this sector is due to the demand for eco-friendly, lighter and high-performing and sustainable materials and products (Anonymous1. 2022).

One of the advantages of using textiles in buildings consists of providing a large obstruction-free span, ease of deconstructing and re-erecting as per the requirements. Depending on the architecture requirements, fabrics can be made into different shapes and appearances. Similarly, fiber-reinforced composites can be made from aramid, glass or carbon fibers to create structures with excellent strength to weight capability, high stiffness to weight and have design flexibility.

Materials Requirements are as follows:

- High tensile and high tear strengths
- Resistant to extension under tension
- Resistant to wind and water
- Resistant to degradation, especially with exposure to sunlight and acid rain
- Low-maintenance fabrics
- Acoustic insulation and thermal balancing functions
- Fire retardant
- Resistant to deformation and extension under tension
- Impermeable to air and wind
- Resistant to abrasion and mechanical damage
- Resistant to microbial attack

Carbon, nomex, wool, polyester, nylon, PP and glass fibers are widely used in buildtech applications. Weaving, knitting, braiding, non-woven and composite technologies are used to manufacture buildtech products. Sometimes, fabrics are coated with special finishes in order to have waterproof functions. For example, polyester fabrics are usually coated or laminated with polyvinyl chloride or polyvinylidene chloride films. Some of examples are insulation, acoustic products, architectural fabrics, glass fiber-reinforced concrete, etc.

Applications of Buildtech are:

Construction of buildings, both permanent and temporary, dams, bridges, tunnels and roads.

1. Tents, marquees and awnings.
2. Architectural membrane
3. Semi-permanent structures
4. Sports stadia, exhibition centres
5. Roofing applications
6. Building and equipment insulation
7. Wall panels, septic tanks and sanitary fittings
8. Glass in bridges

Fig.1.5 Awning

Fig.1.6 Architectural Membranes

Fig.1.7 Tarpaulins

3. Clothtech or Clothing Textiles:

Clothtech includes fibers, yarns and textiles used as technical components in the manufacturing of clothing such as sewing threads, interlinings, waddings and insulation. Clothing textiles forms a part of the technical components of clothing and footwear sectors. Some of the products are interlinings, zip fasteners, elastic narrow fabrics velcro, shoe laces, umbrella cloth, sewing threads, etc. (Anonymous1. 2022).

Materials Requirements are as follows:

- Resistant to deformation
- Good elasticity
- Resistant to extension under tension
- Good dimension stability
- Good seam strength
- Stability to high temperature and pressure
- High abrasion resistance
- UV resistance
- Durability
- Shrink proof
- High strength
- Corrosion resistance
- Light weight

Spinning, weaving, knitting, braiding and non-woven technologies are used to manufacture clothtech products. Viscose, polyester, nylon and PP are used for clothtech products.

Applications of Clothtech are:

1. Sewing threads
2. Interlinings
3. Waddings
4. Insulation
5. Woven and non woven interlining
6. Shoe components
7. Zips
8. Labels

Fig.1.8 Sewing Threads

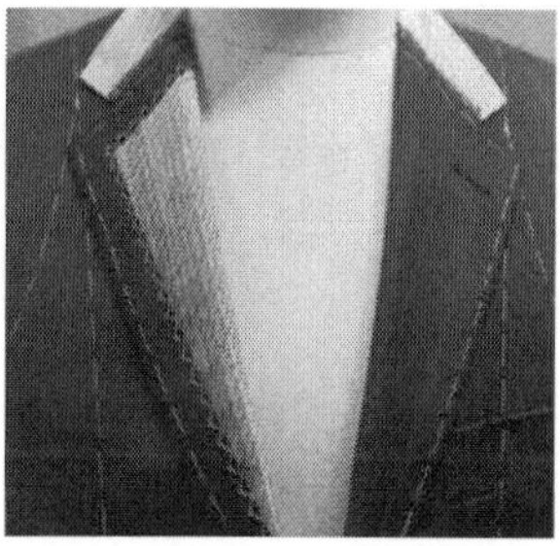

Fig.1.9 Interlining

Fig. 1.10 Shoe Laces

4. Geotech or Geotextiles:

All the fabrics (woven, non-woven and knitted textile materials) which can provide a range of primary functions such as support, drainage and separation at or below ground level, lie in the category of geotextiles. Geotextiles are a part of geotech products. Geotextiles are continuous sheets of woven, non-woven, knitted or stitch-bonded fibers or yarns. The sheets are flexible and permeable and generally have the appearance of a fabric. The mode of operation of a geotextile in any application is defined by six discrete functions: separation, filtration, drainage, reinforcement, sealing, and protection. Depending on the application the geotextile performs one or more of these functions simultaneously (Bhargava et al. 2022).

Geotechnical textiles and Geotechnical grids for reinforcement of base and sub base in pavement structures, Geotechnical textiles for subsurface drainage, sub grade separation and stabilisation, protection (cushioning), permanent erosion control, pavement overlays, slope protection and silt fence Geotechnical textiles for sediment control, Geotechnical synthetic clay liners, gabions for prevention of soil erosion, Geotechnical grids for Geotechnical synthetic mats, Geotechnical nets and Geotechnical composites for waste containment, geo composites / Geotechnical cells / Geotechnical membranes / Geotechnical foams, prefabricated Geotechnical synthetic edge and vertical drains, Geotechnical synthetics for waste containment (Bhargava and Shivankar, 2015).

Materials Requirements are as follows:

- Permeable
- High strength and modulus
- Maintain rigidity and stability to withstand strain, stress, tension and forces
- Resistant to rupturing and puncturing
- Flexible
- High abrasion resistance
- Resistant to contaminated ground water
- Resistant to fungal attack and rotting
- Resistant to UV radiation
- Biodegradable
- Good durability

Geotextiles can be woven, knitted or non-woven and also be made of natural or synthetic fibers. Polyester, polyamide, polyethylene, PP, flax, hemp, kenaf and jute fibers are used for geotech products.

Applications of Geotextiles are:

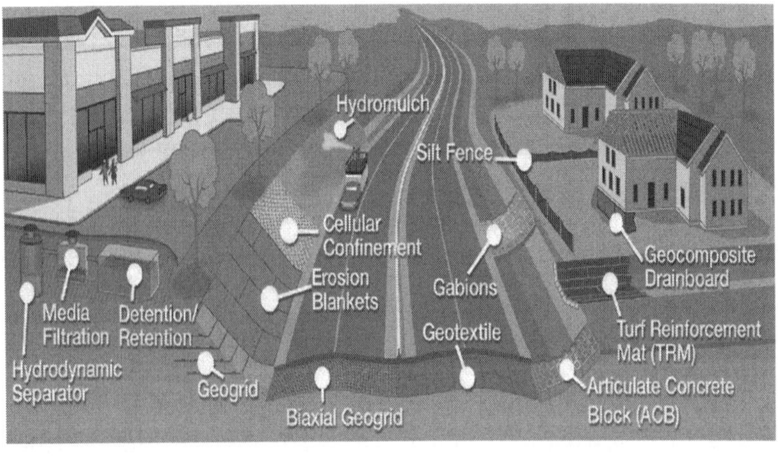

Fig.1.11

1. Geosynthetics

2. Geotextiles
3. Geogrids
4. Geomembranes
5. Building of railway and road cuttings
6. Embankments with steeper sides

5. Hometech or Home Textiles:

It deals with the technical textile components used in the furniture, household textiles and floor covering applications. Some of the examples of these products are carpet backing layers, mattress components, blinds, stuff toys, furniture fabrics, etc (Anonymous1. 2022).

Materials Requirements are as follows:

- High strength and modulus
- Good durability
- Flexibility and good elastic recovery
- Compression and recovery
- High abrasion resistance
- Good handle and drape

Home textiles can be made from woven, knitted, braided or non-woven processes. Both natural and synthetic fibers are used in the manufacturing of hometech products. Acrylic, viscose, wool, polyester, PP, nylon and jute fibers are commonly used for hometech products.

Applications of Home Textiles are:

Fig.1.12 Pillow

Fig.1.13 Carpet Backing

Fig.1.14 Fiberfill

1. Bedding
2. Sleeping bags
3. To replace foams in furniture

4. Carpet and furniture backings
5. Curtain header tapes

6. Indutech or Industrial Textiles:

Indutech includes technical textile products used in the manufacturing sector. It deals with the products used in filtration, conveying, cleaning and other industrial applications. Some of the examples of indutech products are filters, conveyor belts, ropes and cordages, abrasives products, etc. Filtration is a process of separating solid particles from liquids and gases by passing them through the filter media. Filtration is divided into two major categories: dry filtration for air, gas and particle and wet filtration for liquids. Air filtration plays an important role in improving air quality and cleaner environment. Water filtration is one of the ways of improving water quality and safety.

Materials Requirements are as follows:

- High strength and modulus
- Good durability
- Flexibility and good elastic recovery
- Good thermal and chemical resistances
- High filtration efficiency and low pressure drop
- Good dimensional stability
- Good bursting strength
- Good abrasion resistance
- Resistant to UV radiation

Indutech products can be made from woven or non-woven processes. Both natural and synthetic fibers are used in the manufacturing of indutech products. Some of the commonly used fibers for indutech products are PAN, PPS, carbon, high-density polyethylene (HDPE), glass, polyester, PP, nylon, etc.

Applications of Industrial Textiles are:

1. Silk-screen printing
2. Filtration
3. Plasma screens
4. Propulsion technology
5. Lifting/conveying equipment
6. Sound-proofing elements

7. Melting processes
8. Roller covers
9. Grinding technology
10. Insulations
11. Seals & gaskets
12. Fuel cell
13. Conveyor & Abrasive belts
14. Reinforcements for printed circuit boards

Fig.1.15 Conveyor Belts

Fig.1.16 Rope

Fig.1.17 Cigarette Filter Rods

7. Medtech or Medical Textiles:

Textile materials developed and used in medical and hygiene applications fall under medtech sector. Medical textiles can be considered as a part of the wider group of technical textiles. Growth in the medtech sector is mainly due to increasing innovation in medical and textile fields and increasing demand for newer materials with better functionality. According to Bhargava and Shivankar, 2015 medical technical textiles can be classified into four categories there are Extra-corporeal devices like artificial kidney, liver, lung, heart pacer. Non-implantable textile materials like absorbent pad, bandages, compression bandages, plasters, absorbent gauges, lint and wadding. Implantable textile materials like tendons, ligaments, cartilage, skin, contact lenses, cornea, joints, vascular grafts, heart valves. healthcare and hygiene products like surgical gowns, caps, gloves , masks; surgical covers drapes, aprons; beddings (blankets, sheets, pillow covers); clothing (uniform); incontinence/baby/adult diapers; cloth wiper, surgical hosiery, sanitary napkins, medical mattress, sterilization wraps, head and shoe covers, panty shield, wadding; wipes.

Some of the Advantages of Medtech Products are as follows:

- Prevention of hospital infections and cross infections

- Breathability functions
- Higher comfort level, e.g., for surgical gowns
- Engineered to have high barrier to blood and other body fluids
- Compatibility with various types of sterilization techniques
- Cost-effective

Materials Requirements are as follows:

- Biocompatible and sterile
- Anti-allergenic and antibacterial
- Good resistance to alkalis, acids and microorganisms
- Good dimensional stability and elasticity
- Good strength and durability
- Free from contamination or impurities
- Absorption/repellency and air permeability

Medtech products can be made from spinning, weaving, knitting, braiding and nonwoven processes. Both natural and synthetic fibers are used in the manufacturing of medtech products. Some of the commonly used fibers for medtech products are cotton, viscose, silk, spider silk, polyester, PP, spandex, PLA, etc.

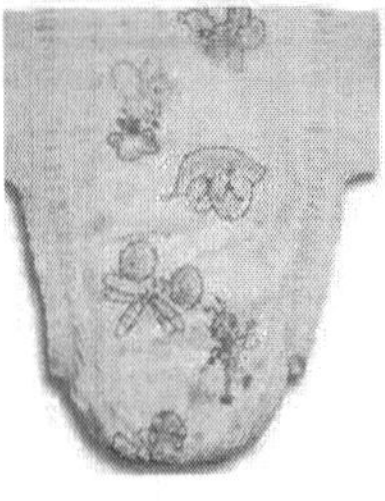

Fig.1.18 Convey

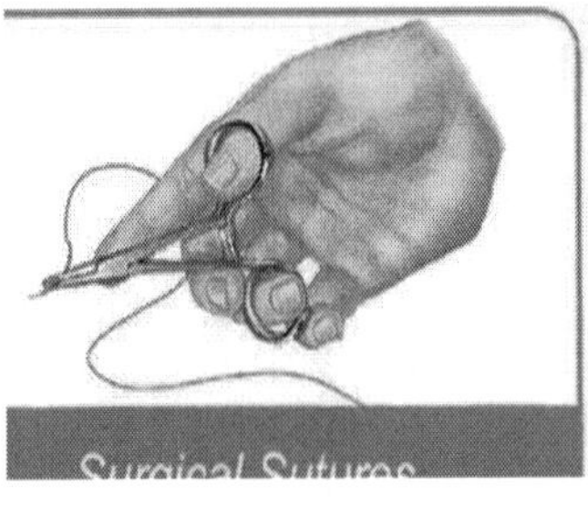

Fig.1.19 Surgical Sutures

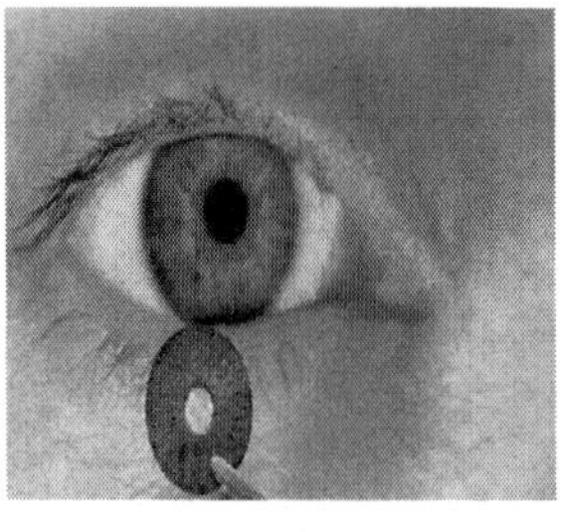

Fig.1.20 Artificial Implants

8. Mobiltech or Automotive Textiles:

Mobiltech are technical textiles used in automotive or transport sector. It includes applications in automotive and automotive components (including aircrafts and railways). Mobiltech covers not only isolation and safety aspect but also focuses on comfort and style. Mobiltech products can be broadly classified into two categories: visible components and concealed components (Raybagi and Nagla, J. R. 2019). Visible components include seat upholstery, carpets, seat belts, headliners, etc. Concealed components include noise vibration and harness components, tyre cords, composite reinforcements for automotive bodies, rail bodies and components, aircraft bodies, wings, engine components, boat and yacht components, bodies etc. There is a variety of functions that each transportation textile can provide. It includes comfort and style for the user, protection against impact, protection against UV rays, weight-saving factors in the aircraft sector, etc.

Materials Requirements are as follows:

- Resistance to sunlight and UV radiation
- Resistance to abrasion
- Good strength and modulus,
- Good dimensional stability
- Reduced flammability and heat stability
- Resistant to mildew
- Ease to clean

Mobiltech products can be made from weaving, knitting, non-woven, coated, laminated or other composite processes. Both natural and synthetic fibers are used in the manufacturing of mobiltech products. Some of the commonly used fibers for mobiltech products are acrylic, nylon, polyester, PP, polyethylene, aramid, carbon, glass, wool, hemp, flax, kenaf, sisal, etc.

Applications of mobiltech are:

1. Car /truck tyre cord
2. Drive belt
3. Cabin filters
4. Seat belts
5. Air bags
6. Truck covers
7. Upholstery

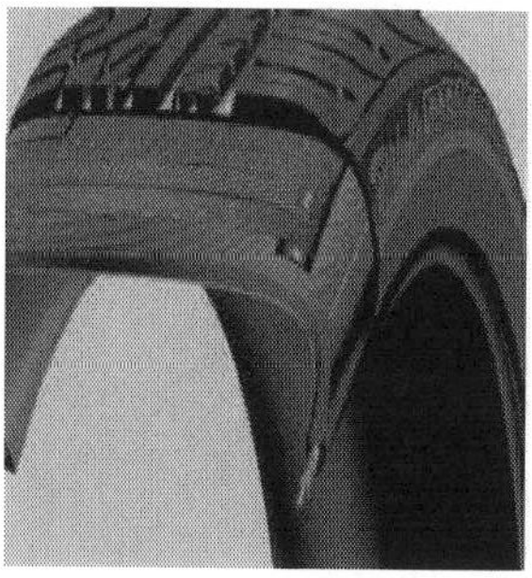

Fig.1.21 Tyrecords

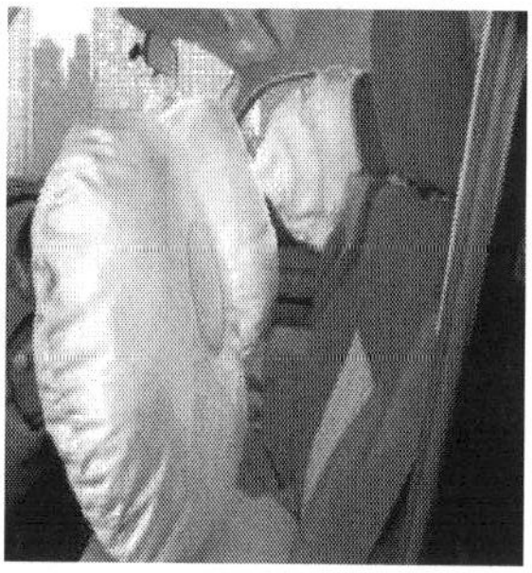

Fig.1.22 Air bags

Fig.1.23 Seat Covers

9. Oekotech:

Any textile product which is produced in eco-friendly way and also processed under eco-friendly limits come under oekotech. Oekotech deals with the technical textiles products used for environmental protection. The oekotech application segment includes concepts in environmental protection, waste disposal and recycling processes. It refers to the use of geosynthetic products to secure landfills against leakage of municipal or hazardous waste.

Materials Requirements are as follows:

- Permeable
- High strength and modulus
- Good dimension stability
- Good abrasion resistance
- Resistant to fungal attack and rotting
- Resistant to UV radiation
- Good durability

Oekotech products can be made from weaving, knitting and non-woven processes. Both natural and synthetic fibers are used in the manufacturing of oekotech products. Some of the commonly used fibers for oekotech products are acrylic, nylon, polyester, PP, polyethylene, jute, hemp, flax, kenaf, etc.

Applications of Ecological Protection Textiles are:

1. Filtration media
2. Erosion protection
3. Sealing of toxic waste
4. Minimising water loss from the land
5. Reducing the need for use of herbicides by providing mulch to plants
6. Reducing weight in transport and construction

10. Packtech or Packaging Textiles:

Packtech deals with the technical textiles products used for packaging applications. Packtech products include the following: polyolefin woven sacks, flexible intermediate bulk container, leno bags, jute hessian sacks, tea bags (filter paper), soft luggage, absorbent meat pad, etc.

Some of the Materials Requirements are as follows:

- High strength and modulus
- Good dimension stability
- Good abrasion resistance
- Resistant to fungal attack and rotting
- Resistant to UV radiation
- Good durability
- Good flexibility

Packtech products can be made from spinning, weaving, knitting and non-woven processes. Both natural and synthetic fibers are used in the manufacturing of packtech products. Some of the commonly used fibers for packtech products are nylon, polyester, PP, polyethylene, HDPE, low-density polyethylene (LDPE), jute, etc.

Applications of Packaging Textiles are:

1. Sacs
2. Packaging for fertilizer, sand, cement, sugar, flour to dyestuffs
3. Wrapping and protection applications
4. Tea and coffee bags
5. Nonwoven insert
6. Knitted net packaging
7. Silos, containers
8. Canvas covers, marquee tents.

Fig.1.24 Tyrecords

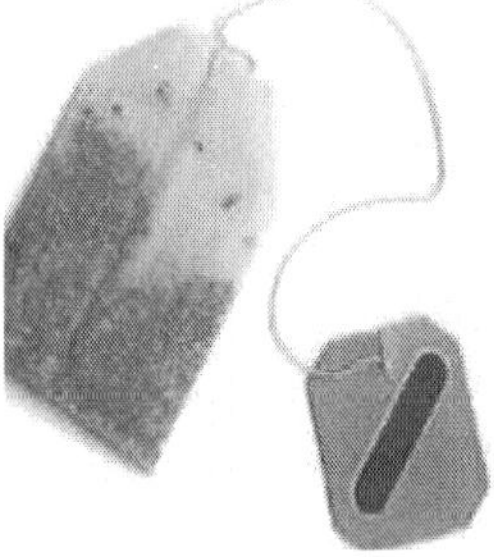

Fig.1.25 Tea Bags

Fig.1.26 Flexible Intermidiate Bulk Containers

11. Protech or Protective Textiles:

Protech can be defined as technical textile materials, apparel, and equipment that are used for protecting personnel and equipment from various environmental and industrial hazards. The variety of protective functions that need to be provided by different textile products is considerable and diverse. It includes protection against cuts, abrasion, ballistic and other types of severe impact including stab wounds and explosions, fire and extreme heat, hazardous dust and particles, nuclear, biological, and chemical hazards, high voltages and static electricity, foul weather, extreme cold, and poor visibility.

Some of the Material Requirements are as follows:

- High strength and modulus
- Good dimension stability
- Good durability and flexibility
- Permeable and breathable
- Lightweight and low bulk
- Good handle and drape
- Water repellent and waterproof
- Windproof and snow shedding
- Heat and flame resistant
- Good impact and shock resistant

Protech products can be made from weaving, knitting, non-woven, coated, laminated, or composite processes. Both natural and synthetic fibers are used in the manufacturing of protech products. Some of the commonly used fibers for Protech products are acrylic, nylon, polyester, PP, polyethylene, aramid, PAN, carbon, glass, polybenzimidazole, Dyneema, Kevlar, SpectraR, ultra-high modulus polyethylene, spandex, flame-resistant cotton/polyester/viscose, wool, cotton, hemp, linen, etc.

Applications of Protective Textiles are:

1. Firefighterer clothing
2. Clothing for welders
3. Bulletproofof jackets
4. Astronauts' suits

Fig.1.27 Fire Retardant Clothing *Fig.1.28 Bulletproof Jacket* *Fig.1.29 High Altitude Clothing*

12. Sportech or Sports Textiles:

Sportech deals with technical textile products used for sports purposes. Some of the sports textiles products are artificial turf, high-performance swimwear and sportswear, parachute fabrics, sailcloth, sport shoe components, sport composites, etc.

Some of the Materials Requirements are as follows:

- High strength and modulus
- Good dimension stability
- Good durability and flexibility
- Permeable and breathable
- Quick drying
- Good elasticity
- Water repellent and windproof

Sportech products can be made from weaving, knitting and braiding processes. Both natural and synthetic fibers are used in the manufacturing of sportech products. Some of the commonly used fibers for sportech products are nylon, polyester, PP, polyethylene, LDPE, spandex, wool, etc.

Applications of Sports Textiles are:

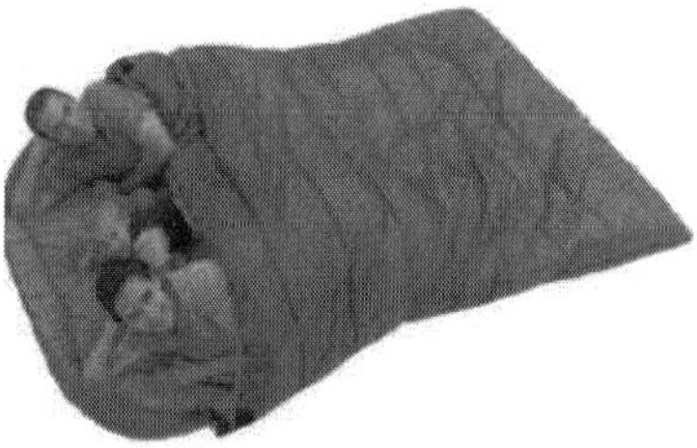

Fig.1.30 Parachute *Fig.1.31 Sleeping Bag* *Fig.1.32 Astro turf*

1. Shoes
2. Artificial turf used in sports surfaces
3. Advanced carbon fiber composites
4. Racquet frames, fishing rods, golf clubs, and cycle frames
5. Balloon fabrics, parachute and paraglider's fabrics, and sailcloth

Conclusion

Indian textile industry is fundamentally strong which can be useful in commodity markets of technical textiles through cost competitive structure. In the high niche market, India has advantage of network of R&D institutions for developing new technologies like Dominance of decentralised sector - inadequate resources and finance, absence of regulatory legislation, absence of required standards on quality of products and codes of practices, deterrents for entrepreneurs: doubt about future market potential of technical textiles in view of absence of regulation and needed consumption, huge capital costs involved for machinery, raw materials and equipment, sustained promotional efforts and substantial investment needed for market development , limited experience in production and use of technical textiles, outdated existing regulatory mechanism, lack of basic infrastructure, skilled manpower, testing facilities, training & educational facilities, negligible investment in R&D on technical textiles, lack of comprehensive database on technical textiles, lack of awareness and benefits of using technical textiles among users, hesitation in accepting world proven cost effective technologies, poor understanding of product properties in regard to its constructability, durability, structural integrity, functional utility, fibre composition and its installation and handling. The value addition in technical textiles is steadily shifting from raw materials and intermediate products to downstream industries where India has a strong base. Low-cost skilled labor is highly competitive as compared to developed countries. The decentralized sector's contribution to technical textiles is significant for its growth in India.

References

Anonymous1. 2022. Different Types of Technical Textiles and Their Applications. Retrieved on 20/11/2022 from https://www.textileblog.com/technical-textiles-and-their-applications/

Bhargava, N.; Shivankar, V. 2015. Technical Textiles – Growth Potential and Prospects in India. International Journal on Textile Engineering and Processes. Vol 1, Issue 2. Pp16-19

Bhargava, D.; Saurabh, and Gautam, D. 2022. Geotextiles. Recent advances in clothing and Textiles. Kripa Drishti Publications. Pune. India

Raybagi, A. A. and Nagla, J. R. 2019. Technical Textiles in Automotive Applications, International Journal of Innovative Research in Science, Engineering, and Technology. Vol. 8, Issue 4. Pp 4563-4571

Chaudhary, A. and Shahid, N. 2013. Growth And Development of Technical Textiles In India: A Comparative Analysis Of Tenth And Eleventh Five Year Plan. International Journal of Engineering Research & Technology. Vol. 2 Issue 5. Pp. 413-428

Patel, M. (2010). Technical Textile in India- A dormant volcano prepares to erupt. Retrieved from http://www.academia.edu/640599/Technical_Textiles_in_India

2. Textiles Engineered Orthoses and Protheses

1. Anitha.B, Lecturer/Garment Technology

V.S.V.N.Polytechnic College, (Autonomous), Virudhunagar

2. Priyanka.R, Lecturer/Garment Technology

V.S.V.N.Polytechnic College, (Autonomous), Virudhunagar

Abstract

The term technical textiles incorporate all textile-based products employed primarily for their pragmatic characteristics, exempting their aesthetic and decorative properties. It is implied that the technical textile is intended to aspect extensive spectrum of certain attributes, making them suitable for extensive range of industries that comprises automotive, aerospace, construction, protective gear, health- care, and several others. Contingent on their purpose, these textiles are destined to sustain enhanced filtration, flexibility, durability, lightness, resistance and strength properties, betwixt other features. In this paper, we contemplate the varied utility of technical textiles with respect to prosthetics. Orthopedics, Orthosis, Prosthesis, Orthodontics and Prosthodontics

Keywords: Prosthetics, Orthopedics, Orthosis, Prosthesis, Orthodontics, Prosthodontics

Introduction

Technical textiles are deemed to be the accelerated growing segment of the textile industrial sector. The manufacture of technical textiles constitutes greater than half of the production of textiles in view of the fact that technical applications are substantially superior to the textile applications. Technical textile industry has perceived phenomenal outgrowth in the recent few years and indeed this growth is computed to strengthen in the subsequent years.

Medical textiles are amongst the most strenuously dilating and flourishing arena in technical textiles. A crucial and major part of the products of the textile industry are employed in the medical, health and hygiene sectors. The applications is found to be enormous and diverse, that range from mere surgical sutures to intricate composite structures for bone and tissue replacement, hygiene materials, protective products used in operation theaters as well as in postoperative wound treatment. The degree of growth and application of technical textiles is due to perpetual progressions and innovations in these fields: textile technologies and medical procedures. The healthcare and medical territories offer the eminent opportunities for the progression of the most refined and valuable textile materials for diverse forms of medical applications and portray as predominant areas for restorative fabrication of technical textiles.

Textile Intended for Medical and Health Care

The term medical textile constitutes all types of textile structures that are utilized in the healthcare system for various purposes. The textile structures used include yarns (monofilament and multifilament), woven, knitted, braided and non-woven textile materials together with textile reinforced composite materials.

The history of medical textiles dates back to thousands of years ago when the progress of wound closures and sutures took place, but the "official" implementation began with the advancement of medical services. With the development of contemporary types of fibres and technologies for the manufacture of linear and two dimensional textile frame works, the construction of textile materials for medical purposes is additionally substantial. Dependant on the application of medical textiles, relevant choice of constituent can be made, initially from the type of polymers and fibres to the shape of the textile structure and the type of textile material. Textile fibres used for medical purposes differ from other conventional materials for the reason that, they must meet certain standards and criteria, as follows:

- Should not have toxic effects on the human body
- Do not induce skin irritation or allergic re actions
- Appropriate mechanical properties
- Good absorption of moisture and water
- Good air permeability
- Biocompatibility
- Bacteriostaticity
- Ability to be sterilized

The major requirements of textile material used in medical are absorbency, tenacity, flexibility, softness and biostability or biodegradability. By employing suitable polymers in the manufacture of textile fibers and materials all these stipulations could conceivably be met. Different categories of fibers obtained from natural and manufactured polymers are employed for the fabrication of this type of textile materials. The most commonly used polymer fibrous materials for production of medical textiles are given in Table 1.

Fig.2.1 Woven Fabric

Fig.2.2 Knitted Fabric

Fig.2.3 Bonded Fabric

Types	Origin	Fibers and polymers
Natural fibers	Vegetable (cellulose)	Cotton Linen Hemp
	Animal (protein)	Silk
Manmade fibers	Artificial (by transformation of naturalpolymers)	Regenerated cellulose (viscose, lyocell) Proteins (collagen) Alginate fiber Chitin Chitosan Polylactide fiber Polyglycolide fiber
	Synthetic (from synthetic polymers)	Polyamide Polyester Polypropylene Polyurethane Polytetrafluoroethylene
	Inorganic (from inorganic materials)	Carbon Glass Metal

Table 1- Commonly used polymer fibrous materials for production of medical textiles

Prosthetics and Orthopedics

Orthosis is interpreted as an external medical device utilized for the sake of assisting, immobilizing or treating muscles, joints, or skeletal parts which ever are weak, ineffective, injured or deformed.

Prosthesis is a simulated part of the body intended to deputize a missed part of the body or to make particular part of the body work in a better manner. Diseased organs such as eyes, arms, hands, legs, or joints are customarily substituted by prosthetic devices.

Prosthesis is termed as an artificial body part whichever completely substitutes the missing part of the body.

The commonalities among both orthotic devices (orthosis) and prosthetic devices (prosthesis) were that both were created to support specified part of the body to facilitate the patient to move or functioned appropriately. Orthotics and prosthetics equally share the similar exemplary specification, that are light in weight, elevated stiffness to shear stress resistance, greater tensile and compressive strength, higher durability under impact, cheaper and easy to don on or off.

The significant dissimilarities among orthotic devices and prosthetic devices is that the prosthetic devices are employed to replace the limb completely while orthotics devices are utilized to enhance the functionality of the limbs which possess deficiencies or deformities resulting in disability to function properly.

General Classification of Orthoses

Lower limb orthoses

- FO (foot orthosis)
- AFO (ankle foot orthosis)
- KAFO (knee ankle foot orthosis)
- HKAFO (hip knee ankle foot orthosis)
- KO (knee orthosis)
- HO (hip orthosis)

Upper limb orthoses

- HO (hand orthosis)
- WHO (wrist hand orthosis)
- SO (sacral orthosis)
- EWHO (elbow wrist hand orthosis)
- SEWHO (shoulder elbow wrist hand orthosis
- EO (elbow orthosis)
- SO (shoulder orthosis)

Spinal orthoses

- SO (sacral orthosis)
- LSO (lumbo sacral orthosis)
- TLSO (thoraco lumbo sacral orthosis)
- CTLSO (cervicothoraco lumbo sacral orthosis)
- CO (cervical orthosis)

General Classification of Amputation levels and Corresponding Prostheses

S.No	Lower extremity	Upper extremity
1	Hip disarticulation	Shoulder disarticulation
2	Transfemoral (above knee)	Transhumeral (above elbow)
3	Knee disarticulation	Elbow disarticulation
4	Transtibial (below knee)	Trans radial (below elbow)
5	Ankle disarticulation	Wrist disarticulation
6	Partial foot	Partial hand

Table 2 - General Classification of amputation levels and corresponding prostheses

Prosthetic Construction Design

The prosthetics are contrived as into two types

6. Endoskeletal prostheses
7. Exoskeletal prostheses

Endoskeletal Prostheses

If the supporting structure is internal, it is termed as Endoskeletal prostheses which are also recognized as modular prostheses that comprises customarily used prostheses. This type of prostheses use the human skeleton as the paradigm and has the tube frame offering the weight bearing activity and a foam cover imparts the prostheses it's near natural appearance. Pylon is a tube frame which constitutes the central part which is also termed as shank. The pylon is fabricated from Aluminium, Titanium or Stainless steel, that connects socket proximally and distally prosthetic foot. The Endoskeletal prostheses incorporate the joint components to aid the necessity of the individual amputee.

Exoskeletal Prostheses

The exoskeletal prostheses are a sort of prostheses where the supporting structures are externally fastened. It is also designated as conventional or crustacean prostheses. The exoskeletal prostheses possess rigid outer shell as a sustaining structure that provides shape and weight bearing action. The weight is beared through the outer shell. It is constructed with wood or rigid polyurethane concealed with a firm plastic lamination.

Fig. 2.4 Endoskeletal prostheses

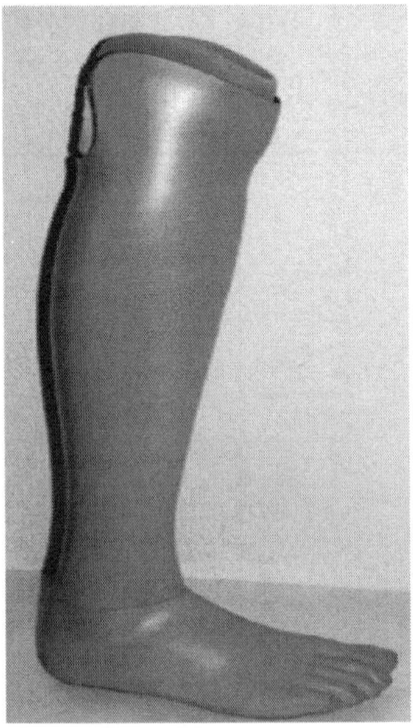

Fig. 2.5 Exoskeletal prostheses

Components of Lower Limb Prostheses

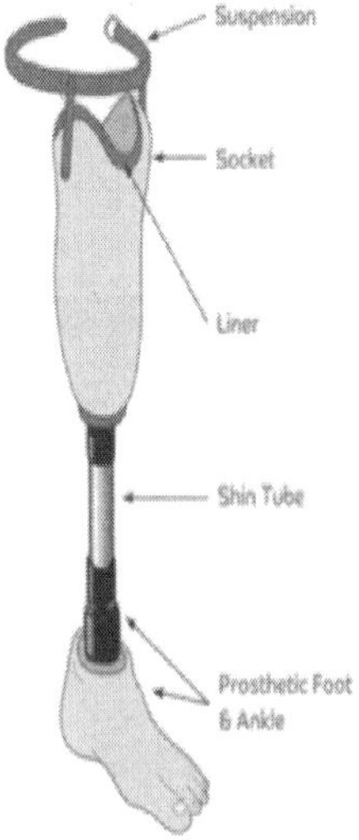

Fig.2.6 Components of Lower limb prostheses

Ankle-Foot Assembly

In addition to providing shock absorption and push-off during walking on even and uneven terrain, the foot-ankle assembly is fabricated to offer a base of support while standing and walking.

Shank

The assembly that connects the socket to the foot-ankle system and transfers the load of body weight to the foot and the floor is stated as shank which constitutes the structural component of prosthesis. It is made of strong and lightweight material.

Socket and Socket Interface

The portion of prosthesis which wraps around the residual limb is termed as the socket is. The socket has to fit always comfortably, enabling the confidentiality to utilize the prosthesis.

Suspension

The suspension is manner by which the socket holds the residual limb. Crucial factor in the design of prosthesis is the suspension system. It enhances the control of the prosthesis, restrict the movement within the prosthesis and curtail any discomfort or abrasions.

Knee Units

The role of the prosthetic knee is to emulate the flexion and extension (bending and straightening) of an anatomical knee joint while the amputee mobilizes. The knee, in tandem with a prosthetic foot, supports the amputee by offering a tranquil gait.

Upper Limb Prostheses

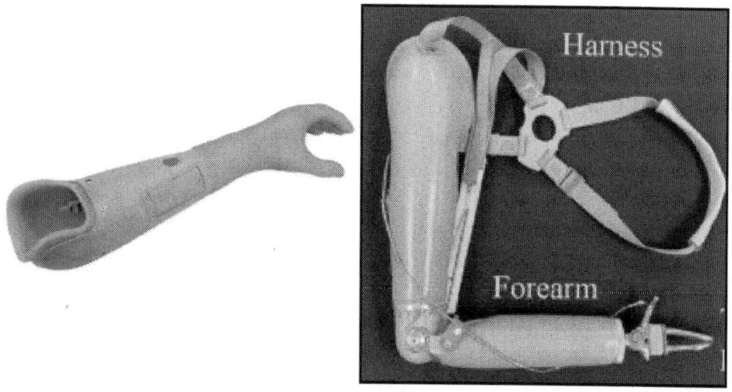

Fig. 2.7 Upper Limb Prostheses

An upper limb prosthesis includes external system fabricated for the partial hand amputation to the inter scapulothoracic (forequarter) level peripherally. This terminology varies from that used by surgeons in characterizing the amputation levels.

Design of Prostheses

The artificial prostheses have to be designed in accordance with the shape of the specified anatomical section. It is imperative that the prostheses require a greater level of customization and designates the interface with the human body. Designing prostheses takes into account, the structure of lower limb prostheses, materials, weight and mass considerations, power requirements, biomechanics, and tradeoffs in motion and stability.

Temporary Prostheses

The temporary prostheses that are termed as preparatory prostheses are employed for early rehabilitation purpose which aid to speed up the recovery process. It is fastened subsequently within few days after surgery. It tends to ease the transition into definitive prostheses. The usefulness of the temporary prostheses is that, it aid the mobility of the amputee postoperatively, preventing the complications of sustained bed rest. Furthermore, it fosters early discharge from the hospital.

Permanent Prostheses

The permanent prosthesis or definitive prostheses is implemented after the surgical wound is healed entirely and the residual limb is shrunk and shaped. The permanent prostheses are substituted when they are worn out and the atrophy of the limb. For efficient weight bearing and movement, the permanent prostheses have to fit appropriately.

Special-use Prostheses

Special-use prostheses are designed explicitly for sports activities that comprise running, swimming, or skiing. They are valuable to the amputee who desires to amplify his activities and contribute to a complete range of sports and recreation.

Materials Used

The varied materials used to fabricate the prostheses should be strong, light in weight, resistant to thermal conditions, prolonged durability, Ductility, stiffness, Elasticity, Density, toughness, corrosion and have to possess biocompatibility. It should not induce allergic reactions to the body.

Prostheses are designed with plastics; the thermoplastic materials which include polypropylene, polyethylene, polyurethane, and acrylic are used customarily. For laminated prostheses, in which the resin is combined with the reinforcing materials like glass fibre, nylon and carbon fibre, the thermosetting plastic is also used.

Orthodontics

Orthodontics is typically among the constituent areas of oral therapy. Orthodontic therapy, routinely delivered by orthodontic specialists, is conveniently available at moderate expenditure and without any risk or complication. It should be accomplished when necessary to enhance the elegance of smile, betterment in chewing mechanism, along with the improvement in self-satisfaction.

Orthodontic and periodontal splints are developed with round or flat metallic wires. But Fiber-reinforced composite (FRC) retainers has been essential, to be used in patients who are allergic to metals or with aesthetic claim.

The conventional FRC materials, due to its Stiffness, could reduce physiologic tooth movement. But a modified construction technique with full bonded and partial composite coverage has been tested and compared with metallic splints which are and found to be appreciative.

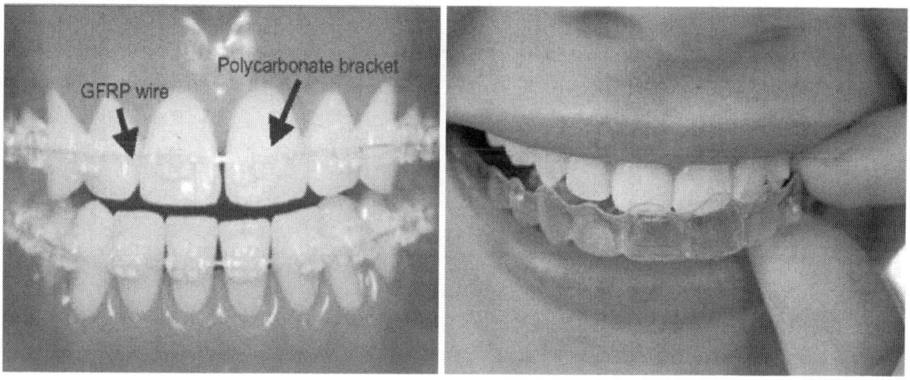

Fig.2.8 Orthodontics

Prosthodontics

Prosthodontics is one of the branches of dentistry which deals with the replacement of missing teeth and are associated with soft and hard tissues by prostheses (crowns, bridges, dentures) which shall be fixed or removed, or may be supported and retained by implants.

The potential advantage of Fiber-reinforced composite (FRC) is that, it offers enhanced aesthetics, low wear of the dentition and the capability to connect the prosthesis to the abutment teeth, which compensates for less-than-optimal abutment tooth retention and resistance form. Two types of composite materials are employed that comprises Fiber-composites which aid to build the substructure and hybrid or micro fill particulate composites to initiate the external veneer surface.

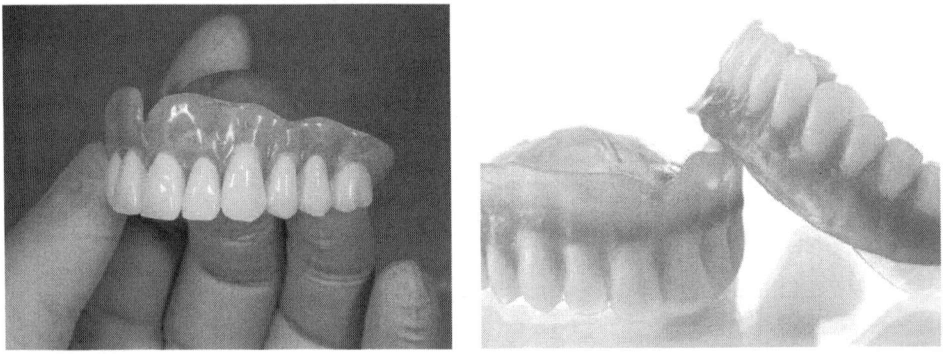

Fig. 2.9 Prosthodontics

Conclusion

Medical textiles, future of technical textiles, play a significant protection role in the healthcare industry. The term 'medical textiles embraces a wide range of delicate goods employed for medical and hygiene applications, comprising surgical, orthopedic, and dental uses. Presently, the application of textile structures in medical field is a flourishing market. There are consistently novel discoveries concerning cellular constituents and the reactions of the human body to new and existing substances. New innovations and advancements are essential as provision to meet the requisites of this new field.

References

Farah Syazwani Shahar, A review on the orthotics and prosthetics and the potential of kenaf composites as alternative materials for ankle-foot orthosis, Journal of the Mechanical Behavior of Biomedical Materials, Volume 99, November 2019, Pages 169-185.

M. S. Wong, Materials for Exoskeletal Orthotic and Prosthetic Systems, Chapter · January 2018 DOI: 10.1016/B978-0-12-801238-3.11040-2

https://pib.gov.in/PressReleasePage.aspx?PRID=1805372

Maria Francesca Sfondrini, Bending Properties of Fiber-Reinforced Composites Retainers Bonded with Spot-Composite Coverage, Volume 2017 , Article ID 8469090.

Mahmud R Ismail, A modified shank for below knee prosthesis, IOP Conf. Series: Materials Science and Engineering 671 (2020) 012061, doi:10.1088/1757-899X/671/1/012061

P. Senthil Selvam, Prosthetics for Lower Limb Amputation, Submitted: September 21st, 2020 Reviewed: December 21st, 2020 Published: May 20th, 2021 DOI: 10.5772/intechopen.95593

3. Microencapsulation Finishing in Textiles

Nimisha Rana

Research Scholar, Department of Home Science,
Dayalbagh Educational Institute (Deemed University),
Agra, Uttar Pradesh, India-282005

Abstract

The development of numerous new cleaner and greener technologies is a result of growing environmental concerns and requests for environmentally friendly textile processing (Melih Gunay 2013). For the environmentally friendly processing of textiles, science has developed a variety of technologies, including microencapsulation, plasma technology, enzymatic finishing, and finishing with natural products. Small solid particles, liquid droplets, or solid-liquid dispersions have historically been covered with thin polymeric coatings as part of the microencapsulation approach. This method was initially developed to support the carbonless copy paper market, but it is now widely employed in a variety of sectors, including the pharmaceutical, agricultural, bulk chemical, food processing, cosmetics, and toiletry industries.

There are many distinct types of capsules and a large range of materials that can be encapsulated. The advantages of microcapsules in the form of over-the-counter medications, such as encapsulated analgesics, are well known to the majority of people. Encapsulation makes the formulations more palatable and less irritating to the digestive tract.

Keywords- Microencapsulation; Textiles; Phase-change material; Fra

Introduction

In the micro-encapsulation process, microscopic particles or droplets enclosed in a coating are used to create small capsules with a variety of beneficial features. The wall of the microcapsule is referred to as the shell, coating, or membrane, whilst the substance inside is referred to as the core material. Microcapsules typically range in diameter from a few micrometres to a few millimetres.

This method is now frequently used for finishing textiles as well. By microencapsulating the core substance, several unique and useful features can be added to the fabrics. Any chemical that will perform a specific function for the fabric can serve as this core material.

Fig 3.1: Microencapsulation structure

Source: http://resource.download.wjec.co.uk.s3.amazonaws.com/vtc/2016-17/16-17_1-4/website/category/2/smart-fibres/micro-encapsulation.html

Moisturizers, healing oils, and pesticides can now be included into textiles thanks to encapsulation. In sporting and medical textiles, microencapsulation of anti-microbial chemicals is also becoming more common. This method has a wide range of applications, including in the finishing of textiles, industrial and agrochemicals, food additives, flavours and essences, pesticides and herbicides, sealants, cosmetics, nutraceuticals, pharmaceuticals, and adhesives.

Microencapsulation, a procedure in which tiny particles or droplets are wrapped by a coating to provide miniature capsules with numerous valuable features, would be a fitting tagline for the practise. While the wall is occasionally referred to as the shell, covering, or membrane, the material inside the microcapsule is known as the core, internal phase, or fill. Most microcapsules are only a few micrometres in diameter.

There are various justifications for microencapsulation. It may be necessary to isolate the core from its surroundings in some situations, such as protecting vitamins from oxygen's deteriorating effects, delaying the evaporation of a volatile core, enhancing the handling characteristics of a sticky substance, or protecting a reactive core from chemical attack. In other situations, like the controlled release of pharmaceuticals or insecticides, the goal is to limit the rate at which the core emerges from the microcapsules rather than entirely separating it. Costs for manufacturing are determined by the coating substance, solvent, tools, and labour. Prices for coating materials vary widely, and often the least expensive acceptable material is employed. The best coatings are those that can be applied without the need of water or solvent.

Objectives of Encapsulation

For one or more of the following reasons, active compounds are encapsulated for use across a wide range of industries:

- Powderizing liquids to reduce clumping and enhance mixing
- Preventing oxidation, heat, acidity, alkalinity, moisture, or evaporation of the active components.
- Preventing materials from coming into contact with other substances in the system, which could lead to polymerization or deterioration.
- Covering up unpleasant tastes or scents.
- Improving how an ingredient is handled prior to processing.
- Release active substances in a targeted or regulated manner.
- Preventing end users or employees from coming into contact with dangerous substances.

Microcapsules Structure

The wall material and the core are the two components that make up a microcapsule. Nucleus material makes up 70 to 99% of a capsule's weight on average. This is equivalent to a capsule wall thickness ranging from 0.1 to 200mm.

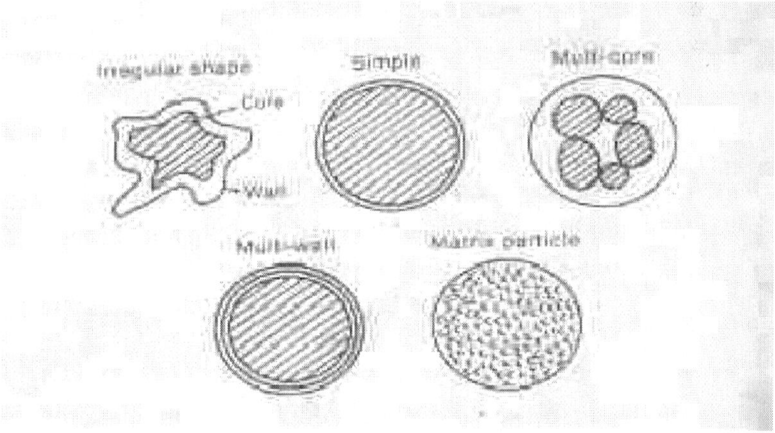

Fig 3.2: Different Shapes of Microcapsules

Source:https://textilevaluechain.in/in-depth-analysis/articles/textile-articles/microencapsulation-technology/

The content of capsules can be released mechanically rupturing the capsule wall, electrically or mechanically causing it to disintegrate, or through a leaching operation carried out in an appropriate aqueous environment. Microcapsules have a diameter that ranges from 1 to 1000 mm; those that are larger than 1000 mm are referred to as microcapsules, while those that are smaller than 1 mm are referred to as nanocapsules.

Characteristics of a Microcapsule

The characteristics of a microcapsule are as follows:

a. **Dimensions and size variation**

Reduced size improves mechanical strength and ease of use.

b. **Loading percentage**

This is the weight ratio of the microcapsule's core to wall; the higher this ratio, the better the production efficiency, but the less stable the microcapsule would be.

c. **Release attributes**

The polymer wall's structure, which is affected by the preparation methods used, plays a significant role in the rate of release from microcapsules. The wall's crystallinity, cross-link density, and porosity all have an impact on how quickly material is released. The release rate significantly decreases as the wall's crystallinity and cross-link density rise.

d. **Thermal resiliency**

The microcapsule should be stable at higher temperatures both during manufacturing and application.

The Purposes of Encapsulation

Materials are microencapsulated to expand their field of action while preventing the environment they pass through from having a negative impact. The following are the main justifications for encapsulation:

- Dissociating incompatible parts
- The transformation of liquids into amorphous solids

A controlled release of active compounds (sustained or delayed release), targeted release of encapsulated materials, increased stability (protection of the encapsulated materials against oxidation or deactivation due to reaction in the environment), masking of odour, taste, and activity of the encapsulated materials, and protection of the immediate environment (Dubey et al. 2009).

The regulated release of active chemicals and improved stability are just two of the significant new properties that the microcapsules may give clothing and fabrics. Its durability is increased by microencapsulation, a special process that enables a controlled release of these qualities as and when needed (Chinta S.K. 2013). Herbal extracts are utilised as the "core material" and the "wall material" in the herbal finishing of textiles to produce a micro-encapsulated finish that is more durable than the other finishing processes. This wall material may be a chemical, such as sodium alginate, or it may be a substance derived from a plant, like gum acacia. When the microencapsulated herbal extracts are evaluated for anti-microbial activity and wash durability up to 20 washes, they perform better. Another widely used application of microencapsulation is the application of capsules containing scent to fabrics. Under typical circumstances, the capsules attached to the materials are resistant to breaking. When pressure is applied to the cloth, the capsules' smell is released, acting as a therapeutic component in aromatherapy.

Textile Use of Microcapsules

1. Phase-Change Substances

Phase-change materials have the ability to convert an aggregation from a solid to a liquid within a specific temperature range. Phase-change material microcapsules lessen the impact of large temperature fluctuations. This makes it easier for clothing to regulate its own temperature and maintain a steady temperature. Different fabrics, such as vests, parkas, snowsuits, blankets, mattresses, and duvets, are used with these kinds of microcapsules (Nelson, 2002).

2. The Fragrance is Over

Numerous times, fragrance finishes have been applied directly to fibres and fabrics, but the perfume does not persist for more than two wash cycles. When applied to textiles, the technique of microencapsulating perfumes prolongs the effect. This method is frequently employed in aromatherapy, where microcapsules may include flavours from essential oils like lavender, rosemary, pine, etc. In essence, this is done to relieve insomnia, headaches, and to stop unpleasant odour.

3. Anti-Fire Agents

To solve the issue of diminished softness brought on by the direct application of fire retardant materials, microcapsules with a fire retardant core were created. They are employed on materials for military purposes, such as tentage (Nelson, 2002).

4. Microcapsules that are Thermochromic and Polychromic (Colour-Changing Technology)

The thermochromatic color-changing system changes colour in reaction to temperature, and the photo-chromatic color-changing system changes colour in response to UV radiation. Polychromic and thermochromic microcapsules are used in textiles for product labelling, security, and medical purposes. There are microencapsulated thermochromatic dyes that, in reaction to human contact, change colour at particular temperatures (Nelson, 2002).

5. Antibiotics

Bacteria frequently induce the microbiological degradation of fabrics, which results in the loss of a variety of valuable qualities. Anti-microbial coatings, which can be applied with the aid of microencapsulation, can be used to prevent this issue. This finish is specifically for technical and medical textiles.

6. Counterfeiting

Microencapsulation can be used to combat the imitation of high-end textiles, branded items, and designer goods. Microcapsules applied to label contain a colour former or an activator. By the use of UV light or a solvent, microcapsules break open, the content is released, colour is developed and in this way detection is achieved (Nelson, 2002).

Techniques of Microencapsulation

Discussed below are few of several techniques that are commonly used for Microencapsulation:

1. Spray-Drying

Most commonly, perfumes, oils, and tastes are microencapsulated using a low-cost commercial method called spray-drying. This process involves spraying core particles into a heated chamber while they are suspended in a polymer solution. As the solvent evaporates, the shell material hardens on top of the core particles, resulting in poly-nuclear or matrix-type microcapsules. When using a lot of core material, the enclosed particles are frequently aggregated, which can result in uncoated particles. However, larger core particle loadings of up to 50–60% have been documented. Due to the foul odours and environmental issues caused by a solvent-borne system, water-soluble polymers are mostly used as shell materials (Ghosh et al. 2011).

2. Coating with Air Suspension

This process offers more flexibility and control. While suspended in an air stream that is travelling upward, the particles are covered. A perforated plate with various hole designs inside and outside of a cylindrical insert supports them. To fluidize the settling particles, only enough air is allowed to rise through the outer annular region. The majority of the rising air, which is typically heated, flows within the cylinder, accelerating the ascent of the particles. They settle back onto the outer bed near the top when the air stream slows and diverges, and they descend again to complete the cycle. In a few minutes, the particles go through the inner cylinder numerous times. A wide range of coating materials are available as candidates for microencapsulation using the air suspension technique. In equipment with capacities ranging from one pound to 990 pounds, the procedure is capable of applying coatings in the form of solvent solutions, aqueous solutions, emulsions, dispersions, or hot melt. Air suspension techniques can successfully enclose core components with micron or submicron sized particles, although this is typically done by agglomerating the particles into a larger size (Bansode et al. 2010).

3. Evaporation of Solvent

Processes are carried out in a liquid manufacturing vehicle in this method. A volatile solvent that is immiscible with the liquid production vehicle phase is used to dissolve the microcapsule coating. In the coating polymer solution, a core substance that will be microencapsulated is dissolved or disseminated. To create the proper size microcapsule, the core coating material combination is disseminated in the liquid production vehicle phase by agitation. The solvent for the polymer is then evaporated by heating the mixture, if necessary. A matrix-type microcapsule is created when the core material is dissolved in the covering polymer solution. When all of the polymer's solvent has evaporated, the liquid vehicle's temperature is lowered to room temperature while still being stirred.

4. Concurrent Polymerization

A single monomer is directly polymerized on the particle surface in a few microencapsulation techniques. Cellulose fibres are encased in polyethylene in one procedure, for instance, while submerged in dry toluene. The average deposition rate is 0.5 m/min. Coating thicknesses vary from 0.2 to 75 m. (0.0079–2.95 mils). Even across sharp projections, the coating remains consistent.

Conclusion

Microencapsulation: A New Technology

The ideal solution for the majority of textile applications involving microcapsules would be one that is simple to use, does not alter the inherent qualities of the fabric, and has a shelf-life on a garment that permits regular fabric-care procedures to be carried out.

Despite the fact that capsules can already withstand 25–30 wash cycles, traditional ironing and other heat-input methods like tumble drying can significantly reduce the desired effect. The microencapsulation sector needs to pay closer attention to the opportunities in the textile sector and especially build microcapsules that solve these issues.

Consumers want new and distinctive impacts to be available in the future. But more crucially, the consumer will demand that fabric qualities, such as fresh odour and softness, be inherent in the garment due to an ever-increasing desire for ease. Customers will anticipate that these qualities will endure the entire life of the garment and won't require routine maintenance in the form of the constant insertion of fabric softeners and washing aids. These long-term objectives might be accomplished by microencapsulation. Textiles that encourage "well-being" will continue to find a market as people strive for healthier, more effective lifestyles. Active distribution from microcapsules makes it possible to create textiles that "interact" with the customer, lowering stress levels and fostering comfort and relaxation. The textile industries have focused on creating performance fabrics with added value for outdoor and sporting applications as well as cutting-edge medical textiles over the past ten years.

Microencapsulation can contribute to this ongoing evolution, for instance by enabling the attachment of sensing chemicals to athletic apparel and medical devices, which can then alert the wearer of potential harm or danger. Systems that administer precise chemical doses to treat muscular pain or other more severe ailments can also be created. The possible uses for microencapsulation in textiles are only limited by the creativity of textile producers and designers. Some businesses have shown early success in creating microencapsulated textile finishes thanks to collaboration and technological adaption from other industrial sectors.

References

Bansode S S, Banarjee S K, Gaikwad D D, Jadhav S L, Thorat R M, Microencapsulation : a review, March – April 2010,1, 2,Article 008

Barari M., Majidi R.F., Madani M. (2009). NanosciNanotechnol. 43-48

Bishop, J.R.P., Nelson, G. & Lamb, J. (1998). Microencapsulation in yeast cells. Journalof Microencapsulation. vol. 15(6). 761-773.

Chinta S.K. et.al. (2013). IMPARTING ANTIMICROBIAL FINISH BY MICRO-ENCAPSULATION TECHNIQUE. InternationalJournal of Innovative Research in Science, Engineering and Technology. Vol. 2, Issue 6, 2326-2336

Cheng S.Y et al. (2008). Development of Cosmetic Textiles Using Microencapsulation Technology. RJTA Vol 12. No. 4. 41-51

Dubey R. et.al.(2009). Microencapsulation technology and applications. Defence Science Journal. 59,1. 82-95

Ghosh SK, Functional coatings and microencapsulation: a general perspective. http://onlinelibrary.wiley.com/doi/10.1002/3527608478.ch1/summary.

Gunay M. (2013). Eco-friendly textile dyeing and finishing

Ganesan P.(2012). Microencapsulation of copper enriched herbals for curative garments. Indian Journal of Traditional Knowledge.Vol 11(3). 532-536

In-Cosmetics (2007), Available at:www.in-cosmetics.com.

Jothi Sri S. et al. (2012). Microencapsulation: A Review. International Journal of Pharma and Biosciences. Vol. 3(1). 509-531

Kumar, A.R.,Rane, Y.N. (2004).Encapsulation techniques.InternationalDyer. Vol. 189(7). 14-21.

G. Nelson (2002) Application of microencapsulation in textiles. International Journal of Pharmaceutics. 242 .55-62

Ramya K., Maheshwari V. (2014). Development of Eco friendly Mosquito Repellent Fabric Finished with Andrographis Paniculata Plant Extracts. International Journal of Pharmacy and Pharmaceutical Sciences. Vol.6. Issue 5.

Sudha, Devagiri S., Neelkanda R. (2005). Microencapsulation: an overview. Indian Textile Journal. Vol 115(12). 25-29

U. Hammad et.al. (2011). Microencapsulation: Process, techniques and applications. International Journal of Research in Pharmaceutical and Biomedical Sciences. Vol 2(2). 474-481

US Patent 005232769, 1993, „Microcapsule,Treating Liquids Containing the Same, and Textile Structure Having MicrocapsulesAdhering Thereto.

http://en.wikipedia.org/wiki/Micro-encapsulation

http://technology.tki.org.nz/Resources/Case-studies/Technologists-practice-case-studies/Resistant-materials-textiles/SmartFibres/Microencapsulation

Chemical Finishing Of Textiles- H.Schindler

Textile Finishing- Mars,Atlas & Wooding

Colourage- Mar 2006

Indian Textile Journal – Feb 2007

4. Digitalization of Figurative Motifs and Patterns in Pattu Shawls of Western Rajasthan Through Design Intervention

Shruti Singh* and Radha Kashyap**

**Research scholar, & Prof & Head, Dept. of Fashion & Textiles, IIS (deemed to be University), Jaipur*

Abstract

Pattu weaving is an ancestral craft of western Rajasthan which is practised in Jaisalmer, Jodhpur and Barmer districts. The craft is dominantly monopolized by menfolk of Meghwal community and is categorised under supplementary weft weaving. Present paper focuses on the traditional motifs of pattu weaving that are all woven in the malani pattu shawls. Malani pattu shawl is a highly decorative shawls ornamented with traditional motifs of pattu in small geometrical patterns. The research describes malani shawl and its motifs in detail that are observed during the field survey in western Rajasthan. A comparative analysis is done between the motifs in the shawls of Jaisalmer, Jodhpur and Barmer. an interactive CD was also developed that contain traditional pattu motifs and layouts of garments to create various design patterns. At last this CD was shown to weavers and designers so that they could diversity the products on their own. It was concluded that the weavers were receptive and were willing to diversity the products.

Keywords: Geometrical motif; Intervention; Malani pattu; Patterns; Rajasthan; Shawls

Introduction

Pattu is a dominant craft of western Rajasthan. It is a hereditary craft which is practised in the surrounding villages of Barmer, Jaisalmer and Jodhpur districts. Pattu is derived from the word patti which means a narrow strip (Bhandari, 2005). Pattu are the example of supplementary weft technique in which embroidery like effects are achieved. An extra weft is passed between minimum two to twelve picks. Pattu was earlier categorized under the woollen textile items which are crafted by the menfolk of Meghwal community. Shawls and blanket are traditionally known as pattu which was made from sheep and camel wool in neutral cream, black and brown colour. Twill weave and plain weave is used to weave pattu and rib weave is used to weave the extra weft patterns. Pattu is specifically woven on pit loom without fly shuttle because various coloured patterns are created using different bobbins. These motifs seem to be inspired from things in vicinity such as household articles, birds, animals and have a strong resemblance to motifs in soof embroidery and mandana wall art done in this region (Rustagi, 2019). For weaving pattu shawls, diagonal lines, stripes, zigzag lines, small and big checks were also the common motifs used in designing (Babel, 2004). An NGO, Urmul Marushthali Vikas Samiti (UMBVS) is situated at Pokhran, which is working for the promotion of pattu craft (Sagar, 2015). A large number of weavers from Jaisalmer and Jodhpur are working under this trust.

Objective

- To document the traditional pattu motifs of Jaisalmer, Jodhpur and Barmer district
- To develop an interactive CD and do interactive sessions with weavers and designers

Methods

To study the pattu shawls, visits were planned and field survey was done. Shawls of Jaisalmer, Jodhpur and Barmer were observed and a comparative analysis was done on the basis of type of shawls, motifs and patterns. To study the motifs, observation method was used and the data is represented in the form of photographic presentation. The collected data is qualitative and therefore, the results presented are descriptive in nature.

An interactive CD was developed for product diversification of pattu weaving that contain the traditional and new pattu motifs along with the plain layouts of men's garments, women's garments and home furnishing products. An interactive session was also organised at Weavers Service Centre, Jaipur to promote the developed CD that will further help in value addition of pattu weaving.

Results and Discussions

During the field survey it was found that there are three types of pattu shawls which are *plain pattu, kashidapattu and baladipattu.* Among all the shawls there is a great demand of Kashida pattu as all the traditional motifs are woven in a series of rows thus the cloth is overall decorated with geometrical patterns. *Kashidapattu* is a multi-coloured cloth in which different rows of extra weft is woven in varied colours. The base colour is majorly in black, white, off white and red in colour and the ornamentation of extra weft rows is done using red, yellow, orange, pink, black and green colours. The motifs woven in first half of the pattu are mirrored in the second half which divides the cloth in two identical half. Earlier desi wool is used in manufacturing but from past three decades merino wool is widely used. They are woven in varied sizes. The pattu is drape by young men and women. Kashida pattu is further divided into two types i.e., bhojasari pattu and malani pattu.

- **Bhojasari pattu**: Bhojasari pattu is named after the village Bhojasar. Bhojasar village is located in the Phalodi district of Jodhpur and these shawls are specifically woven in this village. It is distinguished with triangle motifs, where two triangles are facing towards each other at the tip in centre. The border consists of various small triangle and comb motifs with multiple consecutive patterns. Fish motifs are not used in this pattu. On the edge of the cloth, coloured streak are developed.
- **Malani pattu:** This is a highly decorative pattu in which the entire surface of fabric is beautifully covered with small patterns and coloured streaks. These are usually woven with merino wool. The design takes about one week to complete. Around fifteen types of geometrical motifs are woven in malani pattu (Fig. 4.1).

Motifs in Malani Pattu

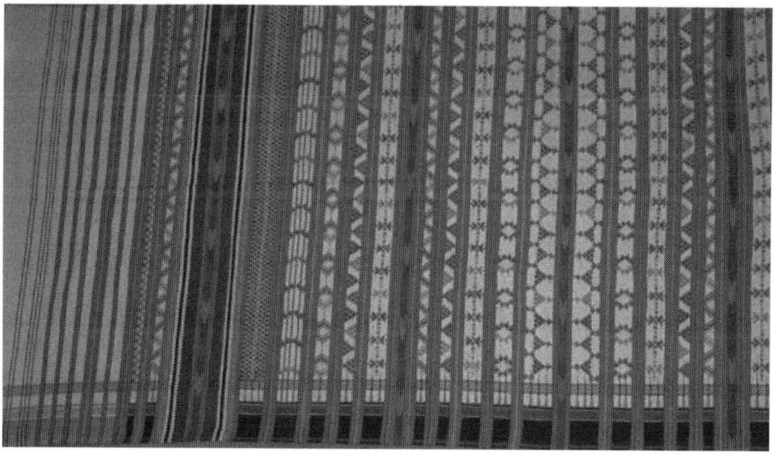

Fig.4.1: Malani pattu shawl

(Source: NGO Urmul Marusthali Bunkar Vikas Samiti, Pokhran, Jaisalmer)

It was found that motifs in the pattu shawls of Jaisalmer and Jodhpur are similar. The arrangement of motifs in pattu is standardized in the malani shawls of Jaisalmer and Jodhpur and they are always woven in a particular sequence. However, the motifs in the shawls of Barmer are somewhat different. and the arrangement of designs and pattern is varied depending upon the weaver's choice. All the motifs used in pattu cloth of all three districts are described below.

- **Do-Dhari**: Streak pattern in malani pattu is termed as dhari which means lines. To weave malani pattu, first of all do- dhari pattern is woven. The term do dhari indicates do meaning two and dhari means lines. To introduce these lines rib weave is used (Fig. 4.3).
- **Teen-dhari**: This pattern is similar to do- dhari but here three lines are introduced instead of two which are equally spaced. This pattern is termed as teen dhari in which teen means three and dhari means streak (Fig. 3). Rib weave is used to insert these streaks.
- **Danti**: This pattern is termed as danti meaning teeth (Fig. 4.2). Danti pattern always starts from the selvedge. The design is between two sevdanti patterns. This pattern is also woven using rib weave.
- **Sevdanti**: Sevdanti pattern is a combination of five coloured lines which are arranged in a consecutive manner (Fig. 4. 2). Here, the first and last lines: second and fourth lines are of same colour whereas; the middle line is introduced with different colour. This design is woven in rib weave.
- **Sankli**: Sankli design is a repetitive zig-zag patterns which is woven using two coloured yarns (Fig. 4.2). Sankli is derived from the word sankal which means chains. This patterns starts from the selvedge where designs are created using extra weft yarns. Sankli motif of Barmer (Fig. 4.5) is different from Jaisalmer and Jodhpur sankli design. In this two triangles are arranged diagonally in a mirror image pattern. This motif is only found in the shawls of Barmer.
- **Mirch:** The word mirch is derived from the word mirchi which means chilli (Fig. 4.2). Mirch motif is a set of two diagonal lines. The two lines meet at the tip which creates the shape of half triangle. The design is woven in two different coloured diagonal lines.
- **Macchi**: Macchi is derived from the word machli which means fish in English. The shape of this design is similar to fish. Macchi motif is the most complicated design which takes more time to weave. This pattern is not woven using extra weft yarns. The weft yarns of different colours are inserted by hands and the pattern starts from the selvedge. Shuttle is not required to create this pattern. To create this pattern rib weave is used and warp yarns are totally conceal by the weft yarns. The design is woven with varied colours and generally four coloured yarns are used to weave this pattern. Macchi design pattern is mostly woven in malani pattu in the end and middle of shawl in Jaisalmer

and Jodhpur. However in Barmer, to make the pattu more decorative, more number of macchi pattern are woven and it totally depend upon weavers (Fig. 4.2).

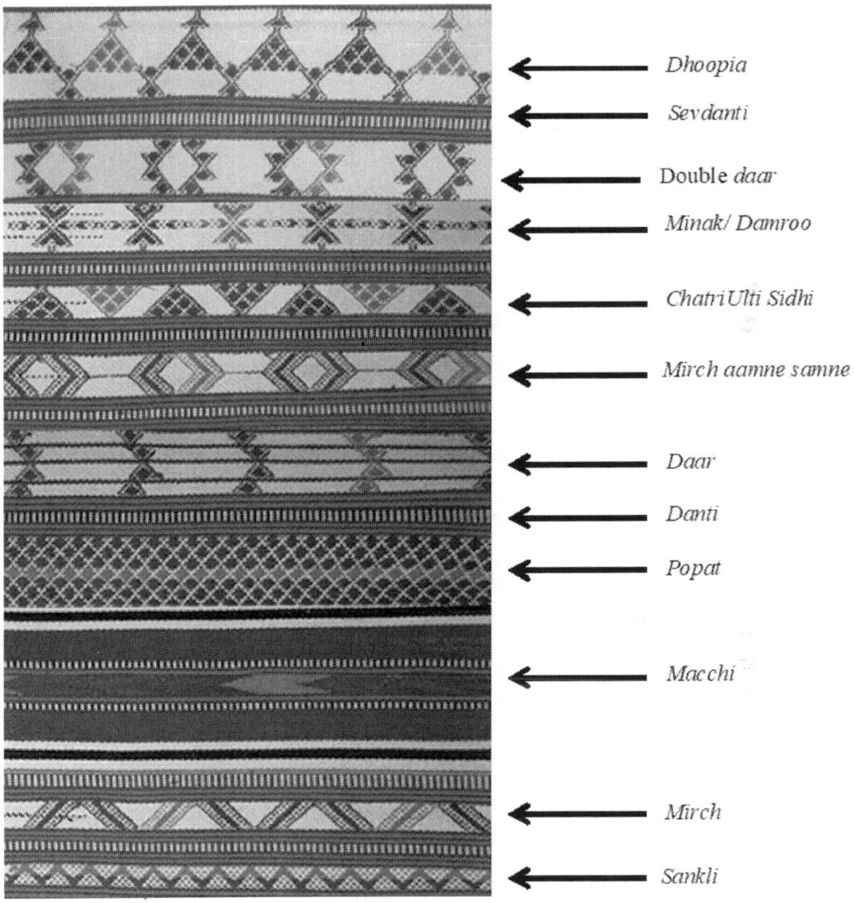

Fig. 4.2: A section of Malani pattu shawl

(Source: NGO Urmul Marusthali Bunkar Vikas Samiti, Pokhran, Jaisalmer)

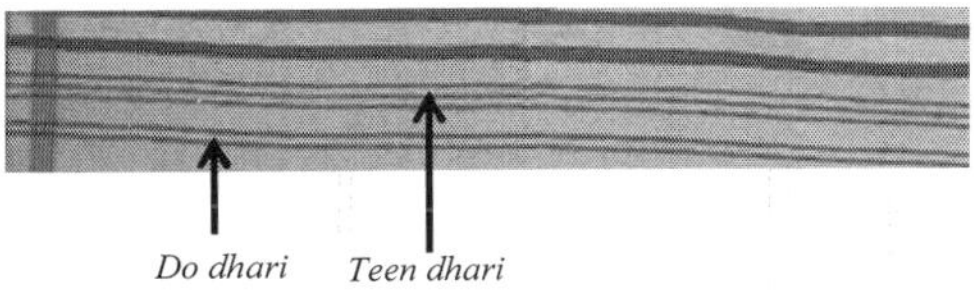

Fig. 4.3: A section of malani pattu

(Source: NGO Urmul Marust Bunkar Vikas Samiti, Pokhran, Jaisalmer)

Figure 4.4: Sankli pattern

(Source: Koda Pura village, Barmer)

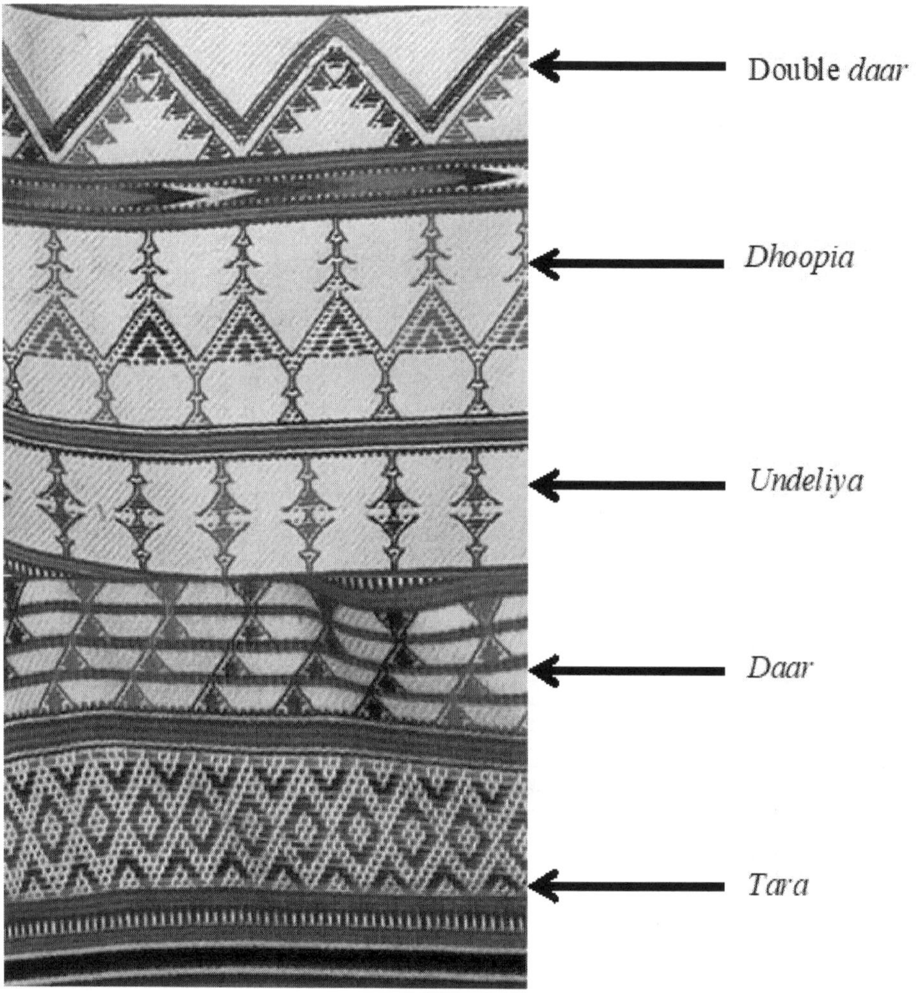

Figure 4.5: A section of Malani pattu shawl

(Source: Bhunia village, Barmer)

- **Popat:** The term popat is used for birds. Popat pattern in pattu weaving is a set of multiple diamond designs (Fig. 4.2). In popat pattern various rows of diamond motifs are woven which are of different colours. Along with shawls and blankets, this design is woven as a border in cushion covers.
- **Daar**: Daar pattern comprise of streaks and triangle designs (Fig. 4.2). When a group of birds fly in the sky creating the shape of V, it is termed as daar. For weaving daar pattern, five lines are inserted which are equally spaced. These lines are usually of same colour. In between

these lines small triangle patterns are woven creating the shape of V. The daar pattern of Barmer is different from the Jaisalmer and Jodhpur. Here the arrangement of triangle pattern between the streaks is different and it does not create the shape of V. It is also woven along with triangle which runs parallel in the horizontal direction (Fig. 4.5).

- **Mirch amne samne**: Mirch means chilli and amne samne meaning in front of each other. Mirch amne samne motif is similar to mirch. In this pattern mirch motif is woven in a mirror image alignment to create the shape of a diamond (Fig. 4.2).
- **Chatri ulti seedhi**: Umbrella pattern in pattu is named as chatri ulti seedhi. Chatri is termed as umbrella in English and ulti seedhi meaning inverse and straight. These triangles are arranged in alternate colours in straight and inverse direction. In one triangle six diamond patterns are woven. This pattern is found in all three districts. (Fig. 4.2).
- **Minak/Damroo**: Minak/damroo motif is a combination of two triangles in which a reverse triangle is woven above a triangle. This motif is named damroo because it appears in a shape of a drum. It is also known as minak which is derived from the word manak. Manak word comes from the dialect of Rajasthan which imply for a person. It is a most common motif in pattu weaving which is widely used in kurtis, bags, dupatta etc. In malani pattu two damroo motifs are interconnected with a series of successive small patterns which runs in the centre (Fig. 4.2).
- **Dhoopia**: Dhoopia pattern of pattu is a combination of chatri and damroo motifs. Dhupia word comes from the word dhuperna. Dhuperna is used to worship God. In Jaisalmer and Jodhpur dhoopia motif is created by weaving chatri design above and between two damroo motifs and a small triangle is woven above chatri (Fig. 4.2). In Barmer, dhoopia motif is created by weaving three triangles above chatri. The chatri motif of Barmer is used to weave this pattern. Dhoopia pattern of Barmer looks more colourful because of the use of five coloured yarns (Fig. 4.5).
- **Double daar**: Double daar comes after dhupia pattern in malani pattu of Jaisalmer and Jodhpur. It is similar to daar but streaks are not inserted and two daar motifs are woven which are placed in a mirror image pattern. Thus, it creates the shape of a diamond (Fig. 4.2). In double daar pattern of Barmer, a triangle is also woven inside the daar motif (Fig. 4.5).

- **Phool**: In pattu weaving, the meaning of phool is flower. This motif is in the shape of diamond. It is mostly used for overall pattern in kurtis, bags, dupatta etc. Phool motif is seen in the malani shawls of Barmer. However now a days, it is widely used motif in pattu weaving (Fig. 4.6).

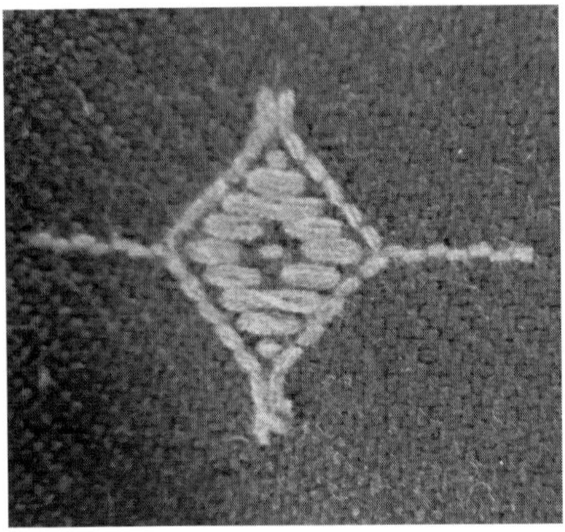

Fig. 4.6: Phool motif
(Source: NGO Urmul Marusthali Bunkar Vikas Samiti, Pokhran, Jaisalmer)

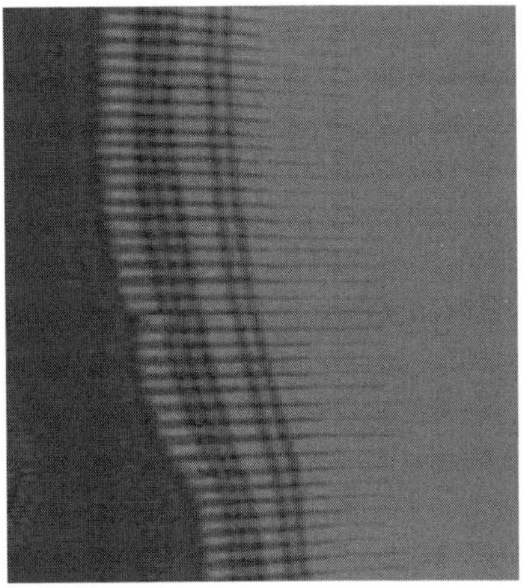

Fig. 4.7: Chotiya pattern
(Source: Indranagar village, Jaisalmer)

- **Tara**: Tara is mainly woven in border. It is created using extra weft which is inserted from the selvedge. This pattern is specifically woven in the malani shawls of Barmer and not found in the shawls of Jaisalmer and Jodhpur (Fig. 4.5).
- **Undeliya**: Undeliya motif is specifically woven in the malani shawls of Barmer. Undeliya means ulta in Hindi. Two triangle patterns are woven in mirror image alignment in the vertical direction. This repetitive motif runs across the width of fabric (Fig. 4.5).
- **Chotiya**: Chotiya is the weaving effect pattern which is created in the border which runs along the length of fabric. Chotiya word comes from the word choti meaning pony. It is woven using warp yarns. This pattern is mainly woven in shawls and blankets. The design is developed in red and black colours (Fig. 4.7).

Development of interactive CD

An interactive CD was developed for the weavers and designers. CD contains Bitmap format of traditional pattu motifs in their original size that allows the person to change their colours. The CD also contains plain layouts of men's garments, women's garments and home furnishing products. By placing these motifs on layouts, one can create various design patterns in different colour combinations.

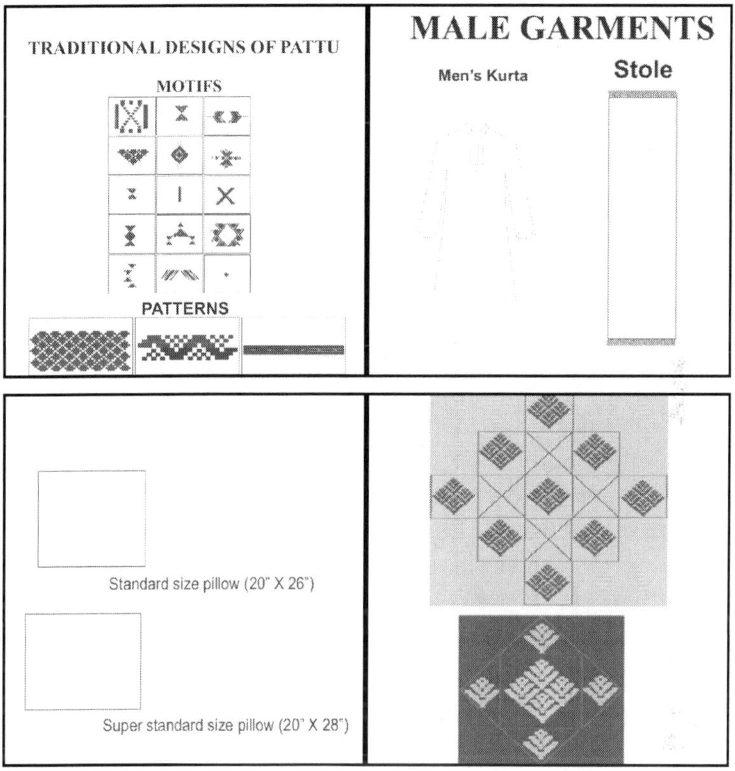

Fig. 4.8: Screenshots of Interactive CD

Interactive programme for Value Addition of Pattu Weaving

An interactive session was organised for both designers and weavers. The main objective of workshop was to explain functions of interactive CD. The developed interactive CD contain line drawing of traditional pattu motifs and patterns. The CD further was developed to create pattern layouts on the fabric for number of products to be developed.

Workshop was conducted at weavers service centre, Jaipur. Designs and patterns were shared with the weavers so as to diversify the products. The purpose of the workshop was to only introduce the weavers and the designers about the designing of pattu weaving so that they could diversify the products on their own and expand the horizon of designing. The intervention CD will also serve as tool to create detailed yet simpler layouts for the products so that the weavers can easily understand them and will perform weaving without making any error which will further result in less fabric wastage. Two days workshop was conducted for the weavers. They were also explained about different layouts that can be created using CD. There were 20 designers and weavers who were benefited by the workshop. On the whole the participants were satisfied with the workshop. Hand on training was also imparted and the weavers explored the interactive CD. They were receptive and were willing to diversify the products.

Conclusion

The documentation of pattu motifs in malani shawls elucidate that the motifs found in the shawls of Jaisalmer and Jodhpur are similar because all the weavers are working under Urmul Marushthali Bunkar Vikas Samiti, NGO and they follow similar motifs that are arranged in particular order of their occurrence. While in Barmer some of the motifs are found in different geometrical shapes with same name such as double daar, daar, dhoopia and sankli. Whereas some new motifs are also found such as undeliya, phool and tara. During the field survey the researcher found that in Barmer, shawls are woven according to the weaver's choice. Because of this all the weavers of Barmer follow different sequence and order to arrange the rows of motifs. However in all three districts, any new motifs past few decades are not found and the weavers are continuing weaving shawls with their traditional motifs which make these shawls unique and distinguish from others.

The design intervention of an interactive CD consisting of layouts for garments will broaden the horizon of weavers and will help them to create other products as per the need of the consumers. The designed intervention CD can help to create different layouts for varied products with a number of colour combinations as the CD contains all the traditional motifs or patterns of pattu craft.

References

Bhandari Vandana. Costumes, textiles and jewellery of India. Traditions in Rajasthan. Mercury books, 2005.

Rustagi, Shalu. "Pattu Decorative Textiles of Western Rajasthan." TCRC- e Journal, (2019): pp. 22-24.

Babel, Sudha. "A comparative study/on profile of urban and rural based handloom weaving units of rajasthan." Phd. Thesis, Maharana pratap university of agriculture and technology, Udaipur, Rajasthan, India, 2004.

Sagar, Purnima. "Pattu weaving of western Rajasthan." MSc thesis, Lady Irwin college, New Delhi, 2015.

5. Naturally Coloured Cotton–Boom for Fashion Designers?

Pradeep Srivastava, Senior faculty, FDDI Kolkata
Levine Lawrence, Chief Catalyst, Ecoideaz Ventures

Abstract

The concept of cotton being grown in just one off white colour is not a fact, cotton can be grown in various different colours like brown, tan, green, etc. Interestingly, coloured cotton is not a recent agriculture phenomenon; it has been cultivated in the northern coast of Peru thousands of years ago. The traditional variety of naturally coloured cotton used to be short staple cotton, which was not very conducive for spinning machines, hence its cultivation was very reduced over the past century. The cultivation of naturally coloured cotton resurfaced during World War II when there was insufficient supply of textile dye stuff.

There is a drastic need to find sustainable alternatives to white cotton and its colour dyeing process. Naturally coloured cotton presents itself as an ideal solution to this major environmental problem. Centuries ago, coloured cottons such as brown, khaki and red varieties were grown over large areas and commercially used in hand-spinning and weaving. However, cultivation of coloured cotton varieties declined later in the 20th century since they were not agronomically viable. Farmers were not in favour of growing coloured cotton, basically because of their low yield potential and inferior fiber quality.

Naturally coloured cotton varieties do have some unique characteristics that make them stand out when compared to regular white cotton. But only some of these unique characteristics are advantageous, while others are quite disadvantageous. They have lower yield, lesser fibre strength and have limited colour variety.

The naturally coloured cotton movement has just begun and it is gaining momentum in various countries including India, China and the US. However, it has a long way to go to become a reality since it is yet to move from research labs to farmer's fields to garment manufacturers. To achieve desired results, collective efforts would be needed from policy makers, farmers and researchers.

Naturally Coloured Cotton - Introduction

Fig.5.1

Naturally coloured cotton is an interesting phenomenon observed in some wild species of cotton. This type of cotton possesses a coloured gene in its fibre that imparts natural colour to cotton as it grows and matures. Naturally coloured cotton grown using organic farming methods is the most suitable eco-friendly alternative to regular white cotton.

While white cotton is the world's most preferred fibre for producing textiles, it is the most environmentally harmful fibre as well. Growing white cotton requires huge amounts of chemical fertilisers, pesticides and water resources. Further, once the fibre reaches the textile industry, it needs to be dyed in chemical-based colours that are highly toxic as well. Evidently, our water bodies and soil are getting increasingly polluted due to white cotton cultivation and garment production.

There is a drastic need to find sustainable alternatives to white cotton and its colour dyeing process. Naturally coloured cotton presents itself as an ideal solution to this major environmental problem.

History of Naturally Coloured Cotton

Coloured cotton was grown and used by mankind as early as 2500 BC, which is evident from excavations conducted at Huaca Prieta in Northern Peru. The coloured lint obtained from these sites show various colours such as chocolate, blue, purple, green, tan. mahogany red, red and creamy-white found in four species of genus, Gossypium. Cotton species such as Gossypium barbadense and Gossypium hirsutum were cultivated in South and Central America as early as 2300 BC. Fibre from these was mainly used for weaving fishing nets, the idea being that the fishes might find it difficult to see a coloured fishing net. It was customary to present clothes made of coloured cotton as gifts the 16th Century AD[1].

In the Indian sub-continent, coloured cottons such as brown, khaki and red varieties were grown over large areas and commercially used in hand-spinning and weaving. These varieties were even grown commercially as recently as 1940s in Rayalseema in Andhra Pradesh. In Assam, cotton with black, brown, khaki and creamy white lint was found. White as well as coloured lints of Asiatic cotton G arboreum have been put to use in the world famous Decca muslins in high count, hand-spun hand-woven fabrics until early 1920s. In fact the Khaki colour was used as army uniform due to easy availability of khaki coloured cotton without any need for a dyeing process.

However, cultivation of coloured cotton varieties declined later in the 20th century since they were not agronomically viable. Some colour varieties had fewer bolls on each plant and their boll weight was also lower. Economically, some have low yield and lint index and technically some have poor fibre strength. short length and irregular colour. The wax content in the fibres of naturally coloured cotton yarns leads to poor fibre strength. Farmers were not in favour of growing coloured cotton, basically because of their low yield potential and inferior fibre quality[2].

Types of Coloured Cotton

Fig. 5.2

There are around 40 different types of coloured cotton. The lint colour is determined by a group of genes that are dominant over the white alleles. Genes for lint colour not only control the colour of the fibre but also other traits such as lint

1 Naturally coloured cotton. ResearchGate

2 Colour cotton research in Mahyco, India

length and fibre fineness. Colour development is also dependent on external factors like sunlight, soil type and plant nutrition.

Genetically, there are two types of coloured cotton - upland cotton and wild species. Upland cotton genotypes are cultivars of Gossypium hirsutum, which are similar to white cotton species in terms of lint length and strength. Scientists in various research institutions have cultivated hybrid varieties of coloured cotton that have the characteristics of both upland cotton and wild species.

The table below lists some of the main cultivars of naturally coloured cotton:

Cotton type	Cotton type	Colour	Uniqueness
Gossypium hirsutum (KC94- 2)	Hybrid variety	Almond brown	Machine spinnable
Gossypium hirsutum (LC-1-1)	Hybrid variety	Dark brown	Best uniformity in colour
Gossypium hirsutum (AD-1)	Hybrid variety	Green,	Susceptible to colour fade
Gossypium arboreum	Wild variety	Brown, tan, white	High fibre count
Gossypium lobatum	Wild variety	Tan, white	Resistant to pests
Gossypium gossypioides	Wild variety	Greyish	Resistant to pests
Gossypium hirsutum (DMB-225)	Hybrid variety	Medium Brown	Good commercial yield

Source: Central Institute for Cotton Research, Nagpur

Varieties and Cultivation

Cultivation of coloured cotton has been attempted by various research institutions and agricultural universities across the world. Apart from these efforts, a few dedicated individuals have also taken up the task of cultivating these varieties and popularising their usage. Here are some of the experiments carried out across the world to cultivate and popularise naturally coloured cotton:

- In 1988, Sally Fox, a plant breeder from Arizona, developed cotton hybrids with long fibres that could be machine spun. She established Natural Cotton Colours Inc. and produced fibres under the trade mark of Fox Fibres. For her outstanding efforts, she was awarded the UNEP award for the environment for leadership in protecting the earth and agro-ecology innovation in Fox Fibres in 1993[1].
- Naturally coloured cotton is harvested in northwest China's Xinjiang Uygur Autonomous Region. China's Xinjiang region currently produces 30% of the world's total coloured cotton grown in a total area of approximately 46,700 hectares.
- In 1996, Jawaharlal Nehru Krishi Vishwa Vidyalaya developed a variety of cotton that produces natural almond brown colour (KC94- 2). This was the first naturally coloured cotton hybrid variety of the country.

1 Rediscovering The Value Of Naturally Colored Cotton

This hirsutum hybrid variety has undergone detailed tests at Central Institute for Research on Cotton Technology, Mumbai and its cotton could be spun to 30s count yarn with quality comparable to that of a white linted variety.

- Cotton farmers at Coimbatore have taken up cultivation of naturally coloured cotton in approximately 700 acres. The cultivating area in Sulur, Avinashi, Pallipalayam, Pongalur and Putharasal and districts of Salem has increased by more than 100 times in five years. T Stanes & Co Ltd an Indian company dealing in naturally coloured cotton of hirsutum type since 1995, plans expansion in this region.
- In India, the Central Institute for Cotton Research in Nagpur (CICR) and several other State Agricultural Universities have taken up breeding programs for improvement of coloured cotton. About 40 coloured genotypes of upland cotton, mostly of various shades of brown and green colour are available in the National Gene Bank of Cotton maintained at the CICR Nagpur.
- Studies conducted by CICR Nagpur showed that fibres of wild species of coloured cotton are weaker and poorer in yield as compared to regular white cotton cultivars. However, some of these wild species are resistant to pests, diseases and are drought hardy as well.

Unique Characteristics

Naturally coloured cotton varieties do have some unique characteristics that make them stand out when compared to regular white cotton. These unique characteristics can be categorised as either advantageous or disadvantageous[1].

Advantages

- **Health Benefit** - Fabrics made from coloured cotton are free of any chemical dyes so are beneficial for both human health and the environment. Workers who work in such production units are not affected by toxic chemicals nor there is any waste discharged into the surrounding environment.
- **Cost Reduction** - There is clearly a reduction in dye cost and water consumption in the textile production process involving coloured cotton. No dyes are used to colour the fabric nor is there a need for huge amounts of water to wash them. However, the higher cultivation cost could negate this benefit, which needs to be studied first in a cost-

1 *Naturally coloured cotton.* Central Institute for Cotton Research

benefit analysis.

- **Disease Resistant** - While the crop yield of coloured cotton is much lower than white cotton, these varieties are disease resistant and drought hardy as well. Most of these are wild species that have endured all kinds of pest attacks, so there will be much less need for pesticides and water irrigation.
- **Colour Intensity** - Interestingly, studies have shown that fabrics made from naturally coloured cotton improve their fastness. Experiments in research labs have shown that their colour intensity increases with each wash.
- **Flame Retardant** - Naturally coloured cotton is inherently flame retardant as its Limiting Oxygen Index value is higher than conventional white cotton.

Disadvantages

There are various negative aspects of Naturally coloured cotton that discourage a rapid adoption in the market. Improvement in agronomic and technological performance in colour cotton hybrids will be required for commercial cultivation and use by the textile industry.

- **Low Yield** - Naturally coloured cottons are cultivated from mainly new hybrid cultivars derived from wild species. Their yield is much lower as compared to regular white cotton cultivars. The average yield is 10 quintals per acre as compared to Bt cotton's yield of 14-16 quintals per acre. Each quintal of naturally coloured cotton fetches Rs 15,000 while the price of Bt cotton ranges from Rs 9,000 to Rs 11,000. So this is a major barrier for their market expansion and popularity[1].
- **Fibre Strength** - These cultivars produce lint that is shorter in staple length and weaker in fibre strength as compared to regular white cotton. So these fibres are not suitable for machine spinning and can only be spun by hand.
- **Limited Colours** - Naturally coloured cotton can only be produced in limited number of colours such as brown, grey and green. So they cannot offer the diversity of colours offered by dyed white cotton.
- **Colour Instability** - When the cotton bolls open up, the fibre colours are brighter but they fade away due to the ultraviolet rays in the sunlight. So there will be inconsistency in colour in cotton lint, leading to patchy

1 *Coloured cotton fades in the face of funding hurdles.* Deccan Herald

look. This is particularly a problem with green-coloured cotton bolls.

- **Contamination** - Cotton is a cross-pollinated crop and the natural colours are governed by a few dominant genes. So if white cotton crops are grown anywhere near natural-coloured cotton crops, then they could get contaminated with colour. Hence their cultivation has to be restricted to a small secluded regions only.
- **Low Market Demand** - Due to the above mentioned disadvantages, there is very low market demand for naturally coloured cotton currently. There are very few established producers working in isolated parts of the world who cater to some niche buyers. Farmers who grow it would have to struggle to find a buyer in their local market.

Comparison of strengths and Weaknesses of Coloured and White Cotton

White cotton	Benefit	Coloured cotton	Benefit
Grown in large quantities across the world	✓	Grown in very small quantities	✗
High cost of production and colour dyeing	✗	Lower cost of production and no colour dyeing	✓
Prone to diseases and pests	✗	Resistant to diseases and pests	✓
Colour fades with each wash	✗	Colour intensifies with each wash	✓
High fiber strength	✓	Low fiber strength	✗
High yield per hectare	✓	Low yield per hectare	✗
Harmful to the environment	✗	Beneficial to the environment	✓

Market Opportunities

Rising concern about environmental problems has persuaded various industry bodies and government agencies to look for alternatives to white cotton. So there is renewed interest in growing coloured cotton and producing fabrics from it.

Since naturally coloured cotton have shorter staple length, they are ideal for producing denim jeans and flannel clothing due to their strong and low maintenance fibers. They can go into any unbleached and undyed textiles such as home furnishings and upholstery. Their duller and natural shades would be much preferred in these textile segments.

Due to their short length and strength, they can be effectively used in the handloom segment to produce premium products with hand spinning and weaving. This can be best exploited in our country which has a rich traditional heritage of spinning and weaving. Further, Since it is inherently flame retardant and UV resistant, it can used to produce flame resistant fabrics such as upholstery[1].

Clothes made from unbleached and undyed cotton are rising in demand in Europe, Japan and the US. In India, too, there has been a steady increase in demand for skin-friendly children's clothing made from naturally coloured fibre. So focusing on kids clothing can be a great market enabler.

However, market availability of naturally coloured cotton needs to be drastically improved before any commercial exploitation can be undertaken. Currently, almost all cultivation is happening inside research institutions, which highly limits the production capability. Even finding seeds to grow is difficult since there are no commercial seed companies supplying these varieties in the market. The only commercial attempt to procure seeds was reported in Karnataka state, where a company named Kandu has collected brown cotton seeds from the University of Agricultural Sciences, Dharwad and distributed to local farmers to grow in a large scale[2].

According to Dr Krishna lyer, Director, CIRCOT, India could become the leading country in coloured cotton if intensive research projects were undertaken to improve its colour yield and performance properties. He emphasizes that more research needs to be carried to improve acceptability of coloured cotton by improving colour and aesthetic value[3].

Conclusion

The naturally coloured cotton movement has just begun and it is gaining momentum in various countries including India, China and the US. However, it has a long way to go to become a reality since it is yet to move from research labs to farmer's fields to garment manufacturers. To achieve desired results, collective efforts would be needed from policy makers, farmers and researchers.

Naturally coloured cotton is yet to make a dent in the large textile industry since it is not even having a market share of 0.5%. As compared to the millions of tons of white cotton produced across the world, coloured cotton is just produced in a few thousand kilograms.

The first step would be to convert farmers to to produce organic white cotton to relieve them of their addiction to chemical-based farming. Once that is done, they will be mentally prepared to adjust to a lower yield and varied hued naturally coloured cotton. As of now, it would be a far-fetched statement to say naturally coloured cotton would become a boon to fashion designers who would like to present a sustainable alternative to white cotton!

1 *Naturally coloured cotton. ResearchGate*

2 *Coloured cotton fades in the face of funding hurdles.* Deccan Herald

3 *Naturally coloured cotton. ResearchGate*

References

Colour cotton research in Mahyco, India

https://icac.org/Content/EventDocuments/PdfFilesb597ad47_8d61_4eb6_8985_dcff30c8bf62/Colour%20cotton%20research%20in%20Mahyco.pdf

Naturally coloured cotton. ResearchGate

https://www.researchgate.net/publication/283581684_Naturally_coloured_cotton

Naturally coloured cotton. Central Institute for Cotton Research, Nagpur

https://www.cicr.org.in/pdf/naturally_colored_cotton.pdf

Rediscovering The Value Of Naturally Colored Cotton

http://www.ideassonline.org/public/pdf/ColoredCotton-ENG.pdf

Coloured cotton fades in the face of funding hurdles. Deccan Herald

https://www.deccanherald.com/state/top-karnataka-stories/coloured-cotton-fades-in-the-face-of-funding-hurdles-1144262.html

6. Recent Developments of Protective Textiles in India

Sushila[1], Sarita Devi[2] and Sunil Changdev Talekar[1]

[1] *School of Fashion Design, FDDI, Noida, UP, India*

[2] *School of Fashion Design, FDDI, Rohtak, Haryana, India*

Abstract

Scientific progress in various fields has undoubtedly increased the quality and value of human life. However, it must be acknowledged that technological advances have also exposed us to greater risks and dangers of being vulnerable to unknown physical, chemical and biological attacks. One such currently relevant danger is from bioterrorism and weapons of mass destruction. In addition, we continue to be exposed to hazards from fire, chemicals, radiation and biological organisms such as bacteria and viruses. Protective clothing is manufactured using traditional textile manufacturing technologies such as weaving, knitting and non-woven and also by specialized techniques such as 3D weaving and braiding using natural and man-made fibers. A common objective of the protective clothing industry is the creative and innovative application of available technology, and much of the technology involved is among the most sophisticated available, and the end uses being complex and of great value.

Keywords: Hazards, Textile, Technology, Quality, Industry.

Introduction

The field of Protective clothing is wide and diverse with each functionality having its own specifications, material requirements, consequent technologies and processes. Textiles of today are materials with applications in almost all our activities, we wear clothes all the time and we are surrounded with textiles in almost all our environments (Wenlong et. al., 2005). The integration of multifunctional values in such a common material has become a special area of interest in recent years. Fibres yarns, fabric and other structures with added-value functionality have been developed for a range of applications (Singh, 2017).

Normal Textile: Fulfils basic needs – aesthetic to simple protection from elements.

Protective Textile: Protection from extreme environmental conditions has always been a critical requirement of textile products. Protective textiles are a part of technical textiles that are used principally for their performance or functional characteristics rather than their aesthetic or decorative characteristics (Subhankar and Pintu, 2022).

Fig. 6.1

Fiber used: Conventional materials such as nylon and polyester, cotton and wool, are also used and provide satisfactory protection in certain applications depending on the hazard or exposure. These types of fibers are used in protective wear developed for impact protection and in textile reinforcement products for different applications.

Techniques used: Protective textiles is manufactured using textile production technologies such as weaving, knitting and non-wovens and also by specialized techniques such as 3D weaving, spacer fabric knitting and braiding using natural and man-made fibers, and finishing technology.

Protective Textile: characteristics

8. **Physiological requirements**-shape, size, mass, strength and metabolic activities.
9. **Biomechanical requirements**-dynamic and behavioral analysis of human activity.
10. **Ergonomic requirements**-mechanical characteristics of clothing should match the mechanics of human body.
11. **Psychological requirements**–Peer group, pride, social and cultural background, aesthetics.

Process flow for design of protective clothing

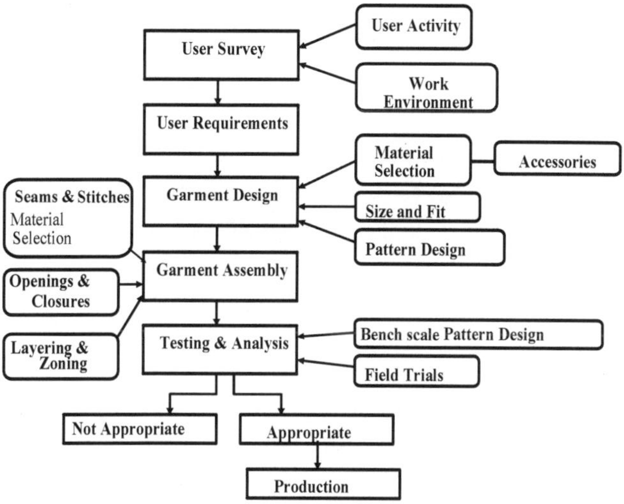

Classification of Protective Textiles:

1. **Flame retardant clothing**: A fabric or product that resists ignition and self-extinguishes after removal of the ignition source.

Fiber used in FR clothing

PBI, Aramids - para and meta, cotton, Coated nylon, Carbon foam, (CFOAM), Polyhydroquinone - dimidazopyridine , Melamine, Modacrylic , Wool, Leather

Advances

Fig. 6.2

Gore-Tex is a functional textile which was developed by Gore for the special needs of firefighters. The concept of this product is to eliminate the conventional, bulky, thermal insulation layer and substitute it by a protective air cushion. This laminated fabric is characterized by thermal insulation, breathability, perspiration transport, y properties and absorption and quick-dry properties.

2. **Chemical Protective Textiles**: The purpose of chemical protective clothing and equipment is to shield or isolate individuals from the chemical, physical, and biological hazards that may be encountered during hazardous materials operations.

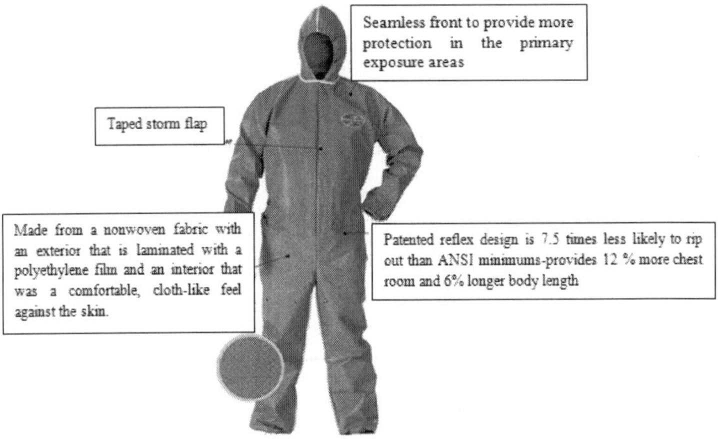

Fig. 6.3

Chemical Protective Clothing is used mainly to prevent exposure during hazardous activities. These hazards can be grouped into categories such as chemical, thermal, nuclear, radiation (X-rays, UV) and biological hazards.

Fibre and Fabric used: Spun polyethylene (Tyvek) and spunbond/ meltbown/ spunbond (SMS) polypropylene (Kleenguard). Microporous film-based materials can be used for chemical protective clothing. Microporous films have millions of microscopic pores per square inch of the film structure.

3. **Pesticide-Resistant Clothing**: Exposure of skin to pesticide is a major health hazard to farmers. Pesticides can enter the body through the skin, the eyes, the mouth, and the lungs (Yadav and Gaba, 2018)

Dressing appropriately and using personal protective equipment can help minimize pesticide exposure and reduce the risk of pesticide poisoning. Protective clothing including coveralls, apron, broad-rimmed waterproof hat, boots, rubber gloves, goggles or face shields, and respirators.

Fibre Used

- Cloths made of butyl rubber,
- Neoprene
- PVC
- Laminated polyethylene fabrics can be appropriate for pesticide protective clothing.

Makkar, 2005. conducted a research on functional clothing for farm workers and found that clothing related problems encountered by male and female farm worker were cut/scrach/ itching on uncovered area of body, soiling of cloth, allergies, breathing problem and irritation. That all prevented by using long gloves, high neck, head cover, proper footwear, using elastic at wrist and pauacha could prevent soiling, face cover of mulmul at nose level prevent breathing problems. Most of functional feature incorporated in the designed garments were highly suitable.

Rani et al., 2017 recommended protective clothing for pesticide applicators were jacket with hood and pyjama of water proof fabric, Chemical Resistant mask, Glasses/goggles, Nitrile gloves and Sports shoes. For threshing activity recommended protective clothing were : apron with hood and full sleeves with elasticized cuffs (elastic in two rows),Pleated mask / beak mask, Glasses/goggles ,Sports shoes, Mittens/gloves (for male) and for female : *Kameez* with full sleeves preferably elasticized cuffs or apron, hood mask/scarf mask ,glasses/goggles, sports shoes, mittens/gloves. They found that the protective clothing/accessories were highly acceptable to maximum number of the farm workers. The designed protective clothing reduced their occupational health hazards and increased their work efficiency.

4. **Mechanical protective Textiles**: The mechanical performance of fabrics is due to hybrid yarns in their interlacing. Textiles for mechanical protection can be manufactured from high strength textile fibres used alone or along with

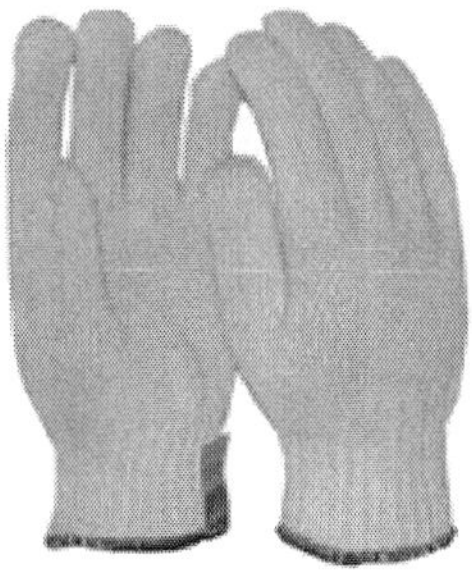

Fig. 6.4 Cut Resistant Gloves

Fig. 6.5 Chain Saw Clothing

Fig. 6.6 Puncture Resistant Gloves

metallic fibres. MPT's have a personal protective function against different risk such as ballistic, blade cuts, fabric puncture, knives, slashing etc. besides combined use of high performance material such as glass fibre, Polyethylene or steel.

5. Ballistic protection: Ballistic protection is a class of protective clothing, which aims at protecting the individuals from the bullets and steel fragments from hand-held weapons. The basic idea of spreading the load over a large area is still applied. It is better to dissipate the energy of impact by deformation and breaking the protective material. Ballistic protection process is a complex phenomenon involving the transverse velocity propagation, tensile properties and the fine structure.

In the recent years, use of ultra-high modulus polyethylene (UHMPE) fibres produced by gel spinning has been started in manufacturing of ballistic protective fabrics.

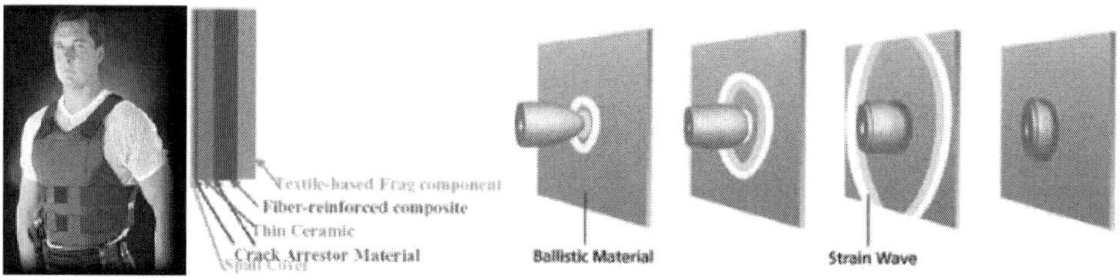

Fig. 6.7 Bullet Proof Vest Components

Fabric Used

- Fabric design is generally plain or basket.
- Nonwovens: Nonwoven fabrics are used in ballistic protection against bullets (police vests, light weight Armour panels, etc.) as it gives a far better protection at the same weight than fabrics.
- Composites and laminates: For non balistic applications, High Performance Polyethylene (HPPE) fibers are mainly used to improve the impact resistance and the energy absorption of glass or carbon fiber reinforced products.

Advancement in Ballistic Protection

Development and use of para aramids, This very high strength fiber, the same as used in tire cord, composites, and the like, is used in soft body armor by loosely stacking layers (16+) of (usually) filament aramid fabric, each providing coverage and progressive resistance to bullet or fragment penetration.

Kevlar® fiber and filament come in a variety of types, each with its own unique set of properties and performance characteristics for different protection needs.

Kevlar® 29 (K29), Kevlar® 49,Kevlar® 100,Kevlar® 119, Kevlar® 129, Kevlar® KM2, Kevlar® KM2 Plus. These yarns are used in ballistic applications, ropes and cables, protective apparel such as cut-resistant gloves, in life protection uses such as helmets, vehicular armoring, and plates, and as rubber reinforcement in tires, automotive hoses, composites for marine sporting goods and aerospace applications

Twaron®, Technora®, Sulfron®, Spectra® and Dyneema® - These fiber offers a unique combination of mechanical properties, chemical resistance, durability and thermal stability. It is highly valued across a wide range of industries for the benefits it brings to a great many high-performance Applications. Good fatigue resistance, Long-term dimensional stability, Excellent resistance to corrosion, heat, chemicals and saltwater

6. **UV Radiation Protective**: UV radiation is a small part of the electromagnetic spectrum which is divided into shortwave UVC (200–280 nm), middle-wave UVB (280–320 nm) and long-wave UVA (320–400 nm). The amount of UV radiation received at the surface depends on cloud cover, geographical position, altitude, ozone layer, scattering in the atmosphere, environmental and related conditions.

The aim of ultra violet protective finish is to reduce a person's UVR exposure. Atmosphere absorbs most of the noxious radiations emitted by the sun, only 5% of the harmful radiations reach to the surface of the earth. UV absorbers such as Benzotriazole and phenyl benzotriazole are able to absorb the damaging UV rays of sunlight. UV absorbers convert UV energy in to harmless heat energy.The UV blocking capacity of a fibre can be improved by incorporating TiO2 into its structure.

Gupta (2016) made an attempt to apply the UV protective and antibacterial finish on two types of cotton fabric, namely, woven and knitted, selected in greige state by using three plants species, namely, Portulaca oleracea (Bichubutti), Syzygium cumini (L.) (Jamun) and Psidium guajava (L.)(Guava). Syzygium cumini was used for application of finish on cotton fabrics as it exhibited highest properties i.e. 19.5% yield , four phytochemicals (tanin, flavonoids, saponin, phenols), 25.01 SPF and moderate antibacterial properties with zone of inhibition of 11 mm for Staphylococcus aureus and 12 mm for Bacillus subtilis, as compared to other two plant extracts.

7. **Biological Protection**: Textiles are known to be sensitive to microbial attack as they have a large surface area and absorb moisture and these factors promote microbial growth. Most natural textile fibers such as wool, silk and cellulosic are subject to biological degradation by bacteria, dermatophytic fungi, etc. Various chemicals and finishing techniques are available that can protect the textile and the wearer from biological attacks. Textiles designed for biological protection have two functions:

Protecting the wearer from being attacked by bacteria, yeast, dermatophytic fungi, and other related microorganisms which cause aesthetic, hygienic, or medical problems. Protecting the textile itself from biodeterioration caused by mold, mildew, and rot-producing fungi and from being digested by insects and other pests (Gupta, 2016)

Chemical finishing is most commonly used for imparting anti-microbial properties to natural and man-made textiles by applying functional finishes onto the surface of the fabric or by making fibers inherently resistant to microorganisms.

Antimicrobial Finishing: Antimicrobial finishing are also of interest for clothing textiles worn close to skin, e.g. socks, stocking, soles, underwear and sport clothing in general.Inorganic salts, organometallics, phenols, thiophenols, heterocyclics with anionic groups, nitro compounds, urea, formaldehyde derivatives, and amines are also used as antimicrobial finishing (Sushila, 2018).

Now medicinal plant extracts from material like Basil leaves, Neem, turmeric, sandalwood, etc are used. These extracts are a pure form of eco-friendly material and successfully application on antimicrobial textiles.

Saini (2014) conducted a study to assess the efficacy of karanja extract on cotton fabric with respect to microbial resistance. Karanja extracts of leaves and seeds in viscous and dry state in two concentrations i.e. 2.5g/l and 5g/l were prepared and four pieces of scoured cotton fabric were impregnated with these four prepared solutions (LEVS, SEVS, SDLP and SDSP) separately. Karanja extracts of leaves and seeds fabric showed very good antibacterial activity.

Sood (2014) investigated the antibacterial efficacy of the aqueous and methanolic extracts of 17 plants which were tested against Staphylococcus aureus and Pseudomonas spp. by disc diffusion method. Aqueous extracts of three plants viz. Eucalyptus citriodora, Pinus roxburghii and Woodfordia fructicosa were selected for application on the selected fabrics on the basis of maximum zone of inhibition exhibited against the test bacteria. Highest antibacterial efficacy on the herbal treated fabrics was observed with Pinus roxburghii extract on all the fabrics.

Rani (2016) reported that Peach leaves extract on cotton fabric is an effective treatment for bacterial resistance. It was found that an increase in the concentration of Peach leaves extract, its zone of inhibition indicating antibacterial activity was also increased and Jamal (2016) reported that Guava leaves extract on cotton fabric is an effective treatment for bacterial resistance.

Nagpal (2017) studied the effect of weed plant extracts and their different standardized combinations on cotton and silk for microbial resistance.

Poonia (2018) studied the effect of antibacterial finish on cotton fabric by using Kinnow peels extract. The antibacterial finish applied with Kinnow peels extract by both methods i.e. exhaust and pad dry cure methods, was highly effective against Bacillus spp.

Conclusion

Protective clothing is now a major part of textiles classified as technical or industrial textiles. The primary role of everyday clothing is to protect the human body from adverse climate, and the term protective textiles is used when they have been especially developed for extraordinary protection such as from fire, wind, micro-organisms, chemicals, gas, ballistic, radiation electricity, etc. There has been a recent trend to develop these materials from natural resources. Today, the hazards that we are exposed to are often so specialized that no single type of clothing will be adequate for protection. Extensive research is being done to develop protective clothing for various regular and specialized civilian and military occupations. Providing protection for the common population has also been taken seriously considering the anticipated disaster due to terrorism or biochemical attacks.

References

Gupta, V. 2016. UV protective and antibacterial finish on cotton using plant extracts. Doctoral Thesis, CCS Haryana Agricultural University, Hisar.

http://www.teonline.com/knowledge-centre/study-technical-textiles.html. Retrieved on 12.9.2022.

https://www.asme.org/engineering-topics/articles/energy/5-advances-in-smart-fabrics. Retrieved on 10.09.2022.

https://www.persistencemarketresearch.com/market-research/functional-textiles-market.asp. Retrieved on 19.8.2022.

Jamal, Z. 2016. Effect of extract of guava leaves on cotton for microbial resistance. Master's Thesis, CCS Haryana Agricultural University, Hisar.

Maity, Subhankar & Pandit, Pintu. 2022. Introduction to protective textiles. Protective Textiles from Natural Resources. DOI: 10.1016/B978-0-323-90477-3.00023-7.

Makkar, P. 2005. Functional Clothing for Farm Workers. Unpublished M.Sc. Thesis, CCS Haryana Agricultural University, Hisar, Haryana.

Nagpal, A. 2017. Application of weed plants extracts on cotton and silk for microbial resistance. Doctoral Thesis, CCS Haryana Agricultural University, Hisar.

Poonia, N. 2018. Efficacy of Kinnow peels extract for microbial resistance on cotton fabric. Master's Thesis, CCS Haryana Agricultural University, Hisar.

Poonia, N. 2018. Efficacy of Kinnow peels extract for microbial resistance on cotton fabric. Master's Thesis, CCS Haryana Agricultural University, Hisar.

Rani, S. 2016. Effect of extract of peach leaves on cotton for microbial resistance. Master's Thesis, CCS Haryana Agricultural University, Hisar.

Saini, P. 2014. Utilization of karanja extracts on cotton fabric for microbial resistance. Doctoral Research Thesis, CCS Haryana Agricultural University, Hisar.

Singh, N. 2017. Microbial resistance of cotton and silk finish with plants extract. Doctoral Research Thesis, submitted to CCS Haryana Agricultural University, Hisar.

Sood, A. 2014. Application of herbal extracts on covering fabric of sanitary napkins for bacterial resistance. Doctoral Thesis, CCS Haryana Agricultural University, Hisar.

Sushila 2018. Efficacy of lemon peel extract for microbial resistance on cotton fabric. Master's Thesis, CCS Haryana Agricultural University, Hisar.

Yadav, S., & Gaba, G. 2018. Awareness of farm workers regarding health problems and use of protective clothing during pesticide application. Journal of Applied and Natural Science, 10(2), 540–543.

Zhou, Wenlong & Reddy, Narendra & Yang, Y.. 2005. Overview of protective clothing. Textiles for Protection. DOI: 10.1533/9781845690977.1.3.

7. Coloured Cotton: Hope for Sustainable Fashion Industry in India-A Review

Anoop Singh Rana

School of Leather Goods & Accessories Design
Footwear Design & Development Institute (FDDI), Noida (Uttar Pradesh)
Ministry of Commerce, Government of India

Abstract

The textile and apparel industry in India is worth 80 billion US $ as per estimate of 2021 (Anonymous, 2022). It is estimated to grow at rapid rate. Natural cotton colour is a relatively new and high-growth market, sustainable fashion in India. There are three propositions embedded in the products viz., value, profit and people. There is a restriction and limitations of growing coloured cotton. However, the net returns are high besides, environmental and health protection that is being offered by this industry. In recent years, there has been a resurgence of interest in organic and naturally coloured cotton owing to chemical free cultivation and processing practices. Despite the fact that coloured cotton has some limitations, there are a number of advantages in its favour. Our approach helps fashion rethink its production and break with the behavior of producing only for profit. It is increasingly important to think about profitable growth with responsibility. India has become fifth largest economy in the world. Consumer preference for organic fashion is touching new vistas. It will be appropriate to make coloured cotton based industry more sustainable by bringing in suitable policy framework in Indian context.

Keywords: Organic cotton , coloured cotton , natural colour cotton , sustainable fashion , coloured lint

Introduction

Dyed cotton was grown and used by humans as early as 2500 B.C., according to excavations at Huaca Prieta on the northern Peruvian coast in South America (Singh, P., Singh, V.V and Waghmare, V.N. (2000). ICAR-CICR Technical Bulletin). The dyed lint obtained at these sites shows colours such as chocolate, blue, purple, green and light brown. Cotton with naturally coloured lint, other than white, is commonly referred to as coloured cotton. In nature, coloured and white linted cottons are found from time immemorial. Coloured cotton is being grown and used by mankind since 2500 B.C. The Old World asiatic diploid cottons are presumed to originate earlier than New World allotetraploid cottons. Coloured varieties were known in diploid cottons and were under cultivation in Asia, particularly Indian subcontinent, China and Central Asian Republics of former Soviet Union since long (ICAR-CICR Technical Bulletin).

In India, the brown coloured varieties of tree cotton (G.arboreum L.), namely Cocanada 1, Cocanada 2 and Red Northerns, were grown commercially mainly on black soils under rainfed conditions in parts of Andhra Pradesh (Singh, P., Singh, V.V and Waghmare, V.N. (2000). ICAR-CICR Technical Bulletin). The red coloured types were predominant and in high demand because of their better staining properties and colour fastness. Coloured varieties failed to catch on with growers, largely because of low productivity per unit area, poor fibre properties, and colour inconsistency. The order of the day was to increase cotton production to meet the basic clothing needs of the ever-growing population. In recent years, coloured cottons are gaining popularity due to their environmental friendliness. Awareness about the toxicity and pollution caused by synthetic dyes has revived interest in growing organic cotton. The need for environmentally friendly cotton can preferably only be met by organically grown coloured cotton, which does not use harmful chemicals in dyeing and processing.

Types of Lint Cotton

The lint colour of cotton grown commercially is often white. In cultivated species, brown and green colours are most common. Some of the genotypes in the germplasm collections of the U.S. and Russian Republics reportedly have coloured lint with shades of pink, red, blue, green, and also black. Sally Fox of Vresers Ltd. claimed to have developed multicoloured lint, that is, the development of more than one colour on the same lint strand. However, genotypes with multicoloured Lint have not yet been made available to research or produced on a large scale. The two common lint colours, i.e. brown and green, are briefly discussed below:

Brown Colour

Among dyed cotton fabrics, brown is the most common colour. Brown colour comes in various shades, ranging from light brown to intense mahogany red. Depending on the intensity of the colour, it is called light brown, khaki / camel, brown, dark brown / chocolate, dirty grey, light brown and red. The brown colour is found in all four cultivated species as well as many wild species. The brown colour is more stable than the green colour. With prolonged exposure to sunlight, the brown colour also fades, but very slowly. In India, the brown coloured varieties are G. arboretum L. namely, Cocanada-1, Cocanada-2 and red Northerns were under commercial cultivation during first half of the 20th century.

Green Colour

Green is the second most common lint colour in cotton. Green colour is less common than brown and occurs mainly in two shades, light green and green. The green colour is more susceptible to fading and fades faster than the brown colour. Prolonged exposure to sunlight while the boll is opening causes the green colour to fade rapidly, and the colour becomes white, off-white, or brownish. The portion of the lint that is not directly exposed to sunlight retains its original lint colour. The green colour is observed mainly in G. hirsutum, and probably varieties with green lint have not yet been released for commercial cultivation.

Sources of Lint Colour

There are two important sources of coloured lint in cotton. These are-

- Germplasm collections, and
- Wild species.

Collection of Germplasm: Genetic resources are of paramount importance for the improvement of any crop. In India, about 40 coloured genotypes of upland cotton *(G. hirsutum)*, mostly in various shades of brown and green, are available in the National Cotton Gene bank maintained at the Central Institute of Cotton Research, Nagpur. These genetic stocks are both indigenous collections and exotic accessions from USA, former USSR, Israel, Peru, Mexico, Egypt, etc. Among the Asian diploid cotton cultivars *(G.arboreum and G.herbaceum)*, about 10 germplasm lines are also available, most of which have a light brown lint colour in India. Studies conducted at the Central Institute for Cotton Research Nagpur revealed that coloured cotton genotypes are poor in yield and possess weak fibre properties as compared to elite white linted cultivars (Reference)

Wild Species: Wild species are important sources of coloured lint. Many of the wild species of the genus Gossypium, including the putative donors of present-day tetraploid cotton, i.e., G. herbaceum race africanum and G. raimondii, have coloured lint. The brown colour in various shades is the most common. Lint colours found in Gossypium species are listed in Table 3.

In addition to lint colour, some of the germplasm lines and wild species possess resistance for insect pests diseases, drought, salinity and also intrinsic fineness and strength of fibre.

Table 3: Lint colours in Gossypium Species

Continent	Species	Genome	Lint colour
	G.trilobum	D_8	Tan
	G.lanceolatum	AD	White
	G.tomentosum	$(AD)_3$	Red brown
	G.hirsutum	$(AD)_1$	Brown,tan,white,green
	G.barbadense	$(AD)_2$	Creamish, white
Africa	G.anomalum	B_1	Brownish
	G.capitis-virdis	B_4	Brownish
	G.somalense	E_2	Brownish
	G.herbaceum	A_1	Greyish,white
	G.longicalyx	F_1	Greyish
	G.triphyllum	B_2	Tan creamy
Afro-Asia	G.arboreum	A_2	Brown,tan,white
	G.stocksii	E_1	Brownish
Arabia	G.areysianum	E_3	Brownish grey
	G.incanum	E_4	Tan
Australia	G.australe	C_3	Brownish
	G.sturtianum	C_1	Brownish
	G.robinsonii	C_2	Greyish
	G.sturtianum var.nandewarense	C_{1-n}	Greyish
America	G.aridum	D_4	Brown
	G.armourianum	D_{2-1}	Brownish
	G.darwinii	AD	Brownish
	G.mustelinum	AD	Brownish
	G.gossypioides	D_6	Greyish
	G.harknessii	D_{2-2}	Greyish
	G.laxum	D_9	Tan
	G.lobatum	D_7	Tan, white

Source: ICAR-CICR Technical Bulletin

Development of Lint Colour

The colour of lint is a genetically controlled trait. The accumulation of pigment in the lumen of lint begins before the boll bursts. In upland cotton (G.hirsutum), pigmentation in the developing lint begins 32 days after fertilisation and it takes nearly six days for colour to develop. In Asian cotton (G. arboreum), colour pigments are observed 46-47 days after fertilisation, and it takes 5-6 days for colour development. However, full expression of lint colour does not occur until the boll bursts open and the lint is exposed to sunlight. It takes about a week for the lint to fully develop its natural colour. The intensity and time required for the colour to fully develop varies with the genetic background of the genotypes. It is interesting to note that while sunlight is essential for colour development, continuous exposure leads to colour fading.

Effect of Sunlight and Washing on Lint Colour

The colour of the lint is affected by sunlight and the colour of the fabric is affected by washing. These two factors in relation to lint/fabric colour are discussed below:

Influence of Sunlight: As mentioned earlier, lint colour is greatly influenced by sunlight. Natural colours are not stable and do not last long. When coloured lint is exposed to sunlight, the colour fades. If green lint is exposed to sunlight for a long time while the bolls are opening, the colour of the lint will fade quickly.The green colour turns to white or pale white. However, the parts of the boll that are not directly exposed to sunlight retain the original colour of the lint. The green colour fades faster than the brown colour. The brown colour also fades, but very slowly.

Effect of Washing: Natural colours react quite differently to washing than synthetic colours. Dyed fabrics fade more or less with each wash. In contrast, fabrics made from naturally dyed cotton improve in fastness and colour intensity with each wash. Experiments have shown that washing fabrics made of dyed cotton intensifies their colour. The idea that natural colour becomes more intense with exposure to sunlight may be true for certain colours, but it certainly does not apply to all colours of cotton.

Advantages of Natural Cotton

Naturally coloured cottons have several advantages over white varieties. These are discussed briefly below:

Human Health effects: Cottons containing artificial dyes have been reported to have adverse effects on skin and human health. Artificial dyes cause allergies and itching on the skin and can sometimes cause skin cancer. In cotton mills, many workers come into contact with artificial dyes. Artificial dyes have negative effects on their health. People who regularly come into contact with artificial dyes are at risk of skin cancer. It is known that most of the dyes used in the textile industry are carcinogenic. The fabric made from naturally dyed cotton fibres is free from such negative effects. If the fabric is made of naturally dyed cotton, there is no need to use artificial dyes. Such fabrics can be safely used even by people with sensitive skin. It has been shown that fabrics made from dyed cotton are best for human health

Effects on the Environment: Various artificial dyes are used to dye fabrics made from white lint. After dyeing, the chemical residues in the form of dyeing or finishing agents are thrown into the nearby rivers and pollute water and soil. This is one of the main sources of environmental pollution. No artificial dyes are required in the production of fabrics from naturally dyed fibres. Therefore, the residues of artificial dyes do not accumulate in the drains. Thus, the use of naturally dyed cotton helps to reduce pollution caused by artificial dyes.

Impact on the Cost of Fabric Production: The dyeing process increases the cost of fabric production. The dyeing process is eliminated when naturally dyed lint is used to make the fabric. So by using naturally dyed cotton, the production cost of fabric can be reduced to some extent. If a higher price is paid for dyed cotton than for white cotton, the reduction in production costs caused by the elimination of the dyeing process is offset by the higher price of dyed cotton fabric.

Limitation of Coloured Cotton

Naturally coloured cottons have some inherent drawbacks. These are: low yield potential, poor fibre properties, limited colours, instability of colours, contamination of white cotton, low market demand, and lack of marketing facilities.

Low Yield Potential: The yield potential of currently available coloured cotton genotypes is very low. The yield potential is almost half that of the white coloured varieties. Because of the low yield potential, naturally coloured cotton has not been able to gain acceptance for commercial cultivation. In other words, the low yield potential of naturally coloured cotton has hindered the expansion of its cultivation. Its cultivation is limited to small areas in tribal regions.

Poor Fibre Properties: The fibres of natural coloured cotton genotypes are of very poor quality compared to white cotton. Natural coloured cotton usually has shorter staple length, lower fibre strength, and low micronaire value. They also have low fibre maturity compared to white cotton. There is a need to improve the fibre properties of coloured cotton, especially fibre strength, to make it suitable for high-speed spinning.

Limited Colours: Naturally coloured cotton genotypes currently available in germplasm have limited lint colours. There are only two colours, namely brown in various shades and green. With only two colours, naturally dyed cotton cannot compete with white cotton because different colour treatments and shades can easily be transferred to white cotton.

Instability of Colours: The colour of naturally dyed cotton is not stable and durable. All colours fade in sunlight. In sunlight, green colour fades faster than brown colour. The brown colour also fades, but very slowly. The green fluff exposed to sunlight turns almost white, while the part covered with the spike (at the bottom of the coil) remains dark green, contamination. Natural lint colour is determined by dominant/incomplete dominant genes. Green colour is controlled by one gene, brown colour by two or more genes. Cotton is a commonly cross-pollinated crop. Under natural conditions, the proportion of cross-pollination is 5-20%. Growing coloured and white cotton in close proximity increases the likelihood of contamination of white coloured genotypes with coloured genotypes and vice versa. Contamination can occur in three ways, namely (1) through natural outcrossing with white cotton, (2) during ginning, and (3) during dyeing. Cultivation of white cotton in the field where coloured cotton was grown in the previous year can also lead to contamination by outgrowth. Therefore, the cultivation of coloured cotton should be limited to small areas only. In addition, research on coloured cotton should be limited to a few research centres to avoid contamination of white cotton.

Development of coloured varieties in India

In India, coloured cotton varieties were released in Asiatic Cotton (*G.arboreum L.)* in the first half of the 20th century. Three varieties, namely Cocanada 1, Cocanada 2 and Red Northerns, were released for commercial cultivation in parts of Andhra Pradesh. Subsequently, work on coloured cotton was discontinued due to its low yield and poor fibre properties. Recently, work on coloured cotton has picked up again. The Central Institute of Cotton Research, Nagpur, and several state agricultural universities have launched breeding programmes to improve coloured cotton. Improvement efforts are focused on improving fibre length, fibre strength, fibre maturity and yield increases. Research on variety development and identification of promising hybrids is underway. As a result of concerted variety development efforts, a highland cotton variety KC 94-2 has been released for commercial cultivation since 1990 by the Jawaharlal Nehru Krishi Vishwa Vidyalaya, Khandwa campus in 1996. Efforts are being made in several other cotton research centres to identify coloured cotton varieties and hybrids with high yield and improved fibre properties.

Performance of Some Brown Coloured Hybrids of G. *Hirsutum*

Northern India Textiles Research Association, Ghaziabad also grows coloured cotton on an area of 10 hectares. Camel brown and olive green naturally coloured cotton of G. hirsutum L. variety are grown and various studies have been carried out in recent years to develop different colour varieties with different chemicals and performance characteristics. CICR had set a target to grow 5000 - 10000 bales of dyed cotton in 2005 out of the total annual production of 1.5 million bales.

Table 4. Performance of brown coloured hybrids

Hybrid	Seed Cotton yield (g/pt.)	Boll Wt.(g)	G.O.T (%)	2.5 % span length (mm)	Uniformity Ratio (%)	Micronaire Value	Maturity Coefficient	Strength 'o' gauge (g/tex)
Vikram x LC1-1	207.8	4.2	33.0	20.7	46	3.1	0.76	37.1
MCU5 x LC1-1	195.3	3.7	34.7	23.3	45	2.7	0.62	36.3
CNH 36 x LC1-1	174.7	4.0	36.2	22.8	45	3.4	0.78	40.7
Vikram x Parbhani American	170.3	3.6	38.0	21.4	42	3.1	0.73	37.7
CNH 36 x Parbhani American	169.5	2.8	37.0	19.3	44	3.1	0.76	37.6
Vikram x Arkansas Green	159.5	3.6	32.2	22.6	47	2.7	0.60	46.6
Vikram x Extreme Okra Leaf	140.0	4.0	36.2	22.2	47	3.2	0.73	39.2
CNH 36 x Extreme Okra Leaf	135.3	3.2	35.6	22.2	42	3.6	0.76	41.4
MCU 5 x Arkansas Green Lint	133.1	2.8	37.5	28.4	48	3.2	0.74	39.6
LRK 516 x LC1-1	130.3	3.5	37.0	24.4	40	2.5	0.57	37.2
MCU 5 x Parbhani American	130.0	3.8	35.0	22.2	46	2.8	0.62	37.6
LRA 5166 (Check)	173.3	3.2	34.2	25.7	46	3.4	0.77	45.3

Source: ICAR-CICR Technical Bulletin

Limitations for Future

The limitations which impede commercial cultivation of coloured cotton, itself signalize future thrust area of research. These are as follows:

- Development of wide range of colours with different shades, uniformity and stability.
- Improvement of fibre properties such as length, strength and maturity.

- Development of high yielding, early maturing varieties and hybrids.
- Development of coloured cotton varieties and hybrids amenable to mechanical picking.
- Development of male sterility based hybrids in desi and upland coloured cottons.
- Development of coloured transgenic cottons.

Naturally dyed cotton -Boon for Designers & Sustainable Fashion

Revival Trends

In recent years, there has been a resurgence of interest in organic cotton and naturally coloured cotton because their cultivation and processing are free of harmful and polluting chemicals. Despite the fact that coloured cotton has some limitations, there are a number of advantages in its favour. These are enumerated below:

- Producers of naturally dyed cotton have to use less pesticides.
- Dyed cotton has many insensitive and disease resistant properties and is drought and salt tolerant.
- The wax content in naturally dyed cotton can also be an advantage, as it facilitates the removal of dirt from the fibres.
- It offers alternatives for clean fashion. The sustainable fashion market is looking for inputs for ethical, humane and fair production.
- Natural Cotton Colour is in a relatively new and high-growth market, sustainable fashion.

The domestic textiles and apparel industry is expected to be worth $152 billion in 2021. India's textiles and apparel industry has strengths across the entire value chain, from fibre, yarn, fabric, and apparel. The Indian textile and apparel industry is extremely diverse, with products ranging from traditional handloom, handicrafts, wool, and silk products to the organised textile industry in India. The organised textile industry in India is distinguished by the use of capital-intensive technology for the mass production of textile products and includes spinning, weaving, processing, and apparel manufacturing. In 2019-20, the domestic textiles and apparel industry was valued at $150.5 billion. Cotton supports the livelihoods of an estimated 5.8 million cotton farmers and 40-50 million people involved in related activities such as cotton processing and trade.

India recorded $ 41 billion in textile exports in fiscal year 2021, with a CAGR (2.7) slightly higher than the global average. Japan, Mauritius, Italy, and Belgium are the top FDI contributors to India's textile sector (including dyed and printed) from April 2016 to March 2021. India achieved its highest-ever Textiles and Apparel (T&A) including Handicrafts export total of $44.4 billion in FY 2021-22, representing a 41% and 26% increase over corresponding figures in FY 2020-21 and FY 2019-20, respectively.

Cotton production employs 5.8 million farmers and 40-50 million people in related industries. Furthermore, the $75 billion in domestic consumption was divided into apparel ($55 billion), technical textiles ($15 billion), and home furnishings ($5 billion). While apparel exports totaled $12 billion, home textile exports totaled $4.8 billion, fabric exports totaled $4 billion, and yarn exports totaled $1 billion (Ashtha Tyagi ,2022 ,Invest India). So we can see there is huge potential of organic and coloured cotton in international market .

Conclusion

A surge of interest in naturally coloured cotton in recent times will not only lead to development of handloom cottage industry but it will also give options to organic consumer for chemical free textile. China is leading producer of naturally coloured cotton whereas India has entered in to fray recently. Policy makers, researchers, farmers, industry and designers have to come under one umbrella to push up the Naturally Coloured Cotton Movement in India. India has sufficient infrastructure such as Central Cotton Research Institute, Cotton Council of India, NIFT, NID etc to cater to the Naturally coloured cotton industry.

Acknowledgement

Author is grateful to Managing Direcor, FDDI, Noida for allowing and facilitating to write the review paper.

References

1 Anonymous (2022).Market value of textile and apparel India FY 2006-2026. www.statista.com

2 Astha tyagi (2022) , textile sector https://www.investindia.gov.in/sector/textiles-apparel

3 Anonymous (2022). https://www.ibef.org/industry/textiles

4 Singh, P., Singh, V.V and Waghmare, V.N. (2000). Naturally coloured cotton. Published by ICAR-CICR Technical Bulletin no 4, pp 1-10

8. Functional & Protective Clothing

Annu Yadav, Priyanka Lamba

Assistant Professor, Faculty of Fashion & Design
Shree Guru Gobind Singh Tricentenary University,
Gurgaon-Badli Road Chandu, Budhera,
Gurugram, Haryana 122505

Abstract

Functional & Protective clothing is one of the main categories of technical textiles that represent the fields where clothing is fused in different technologies such as sports, medicine, biotechnology, nanotechnology and other to satisfy the needs of the wearer. Functional clothing is the term used for clothing that is being tailored according to the wearer needs under challenging circumstances. There are a lot of functional clothing availed in the market such as Protect (also known as protective clothing), Meditech (medical clothing), sportech and many more. These categories would all adhere to a similar principle of design for the clothing that fell into each one. As the technologies advances, new and more innovative clothing will continue to emerge in the field of technical textile.

Keywords: Functional Clothing, Protective Clothing, Technical Clothing

Introduction

Clothing is a necessity for everyone, but it has also become a powerful tool for self expression. The fashion industry is a vast and ever-changing landscape, with new trends and styles appearing all the time. There have been periods of great creative output, and also most of the time it is important for developments. However, one of the most significant changes in recent years has been the increasing popularity of functional and protective clothing.

The functional and protective clothing is revolutionizing the fashion industry. In the past, these garments were seen as boring and utilitarian. However, today's functional and protective clothing is stylist and fashionable. This type of clothing is made from high-tech materials that are designed to perform specific functions. Generally functional clothing is designed to protect the wearer from the elements. This type of clothing is popular among outdoor enthusiasts and athletes. Protective clothing is designed to protect the wearer from injuries.

The area of functional & protective clothing covers a wide and diverse variety of products with each function having its own specifications, raw-material requirement, technologies and processes. Most of these technologies used are mostly available at a given point of time. The application for protective and functional clothing is numerous and frequently complex, ranging from those that improves quality of life to those that save lives in dangerous situations.

Definition

All clothing's are recognized to have a variety of purposes ranging from aesthetics to fundamental protection. The term "functional clothing" refers to all such types of clothing that is specially developed to provide the wearer with a pre-defined performance and functionality, in addition to its typical functions. These clothing's are a combination of materials that can enhance the function of the clothing that is expected to perform. These can be clothing's that safeguard people who are engaged in life threatening or hazardous environment during work place or activities. For examples: Winter clothes are often made from insulation that helps to keep you warm, while raincoats are often made often made from waterproof material that help to keep you dry. It can also be clothing that has an aesthetic purpose, such as emphasing a wearer's personality or body type. Additionally these cloths incorporate technological features that can be used for communication and telecommunication. These cloths are also made to be as comfortable as possible according to the wearer choice or recommendation.

Classification of Functional Clothing

The development of these textiles in the industry opens a completely new domain of intervention in technologies. The term "Functional Clothing" is a very diverse part of technical textile in the market. It encompasses all clothing varieties that are specifically created to serve a purpose other than their intended use for the wearer. These textiles are designed and developed based on the wearer's requirements for the materials, the technologies they choose based on intended functionality, and their consideration. There are generally 6 classes that covers most logical types of functional clothing, each class has a subclass, as the final product may find application in a variety of fields:

- Protech
- Meditech
- Sportech
- Vanity Functional Clothing
- Clothing for Cross Functional Assemblies

- Clothing for special needs

This section only covers the functional clothing needs that have items on the market or under development, not all of them. These classes differ from one another in terms of the functionality and design principles used.

Protective Functional (Protech): This segment of functional clothing is one of the largest segments in term of intervention. The term "protective functional (Protech)" implies the clothing that includes protectors which cover or replace our personal clothing to protective clothing which helps us in prevention from hazards and injuries. It allows people to work in a hostile environment, as it improves the quality the life. These protective functional can be sub-classified into 3 categories which includes Environmental hazard protective, Biological, chemical and radiation hazard protective and Injury protective.

Protection Against Environmental Hazard: The main source of environmental conditions, whether they are man-made or natural, including intense rain, extreme cold or heat, UV radiation, etc., is nature. Protecting the body from numerous harsh environmental conditions is necessary in this situation. Good insulation with little weight and bulk would be essential.

Protection against Biological, Chemical and Radiation Hazard: These risks are also prevalent in the environment, but their needs are entirely different from those of the first group. In this situation, it would be necessary to build a barrier to stop chemicals, harmful gases, etc. from ingesting, penetrating, or coming into touch with the skin in any way. The primary materials utilized in these goods are clothes with unique coatings and laminations. Doctors and other healthcare professionals typically wear biological protective clothing, whereas industrial and military attire is made to guard against radiation and chemical threats.

Protection Against Injury: In this instance, the danger is what results in impacts that are mechanical, blunt, and ballistic in nature. Ballistic injuries are the oldest type of high impact injuries from a wide range of sources. Depending on the perceived nature of the hazard, multiple layers of high strength fibers, ceramics, metal sheets, and composites are combined to create soft armor that has the ideal balance of light weight and excellent protection.

Medical Functional (Meditech): Medical gear includes items like aprons, gloves, and patient and surgeon gowns. This category of clothing is also known as "Health care sector". The primary purpose of this garment is to protect the wearer from fluids, pathogens, and other substances that can be dangerous to both patients and surgeons. These goods include several different types of protective apparel. Based on clothes and smart functional apparels, these fabrics have features including absorbency, air permeability, and durability. These media can be further separated into categories, such as Bio-sensing clothes and Therapeutic and rehabilitative clothing.

Therapeutic and Rehabilitative Clothing: The main function of Therapeutic and rehabilitative clothing is pressure theory that imparts through compression garment. These garments are generally used in treatment of hypertrophic scar, burn injury etc. the pressure garments also helps in circulation of blood flow in the body. The rehabilitative clothing is one of the recent innovations in medical functional clothing. This class of clothing is custom made for patients who has unusual body measurements. These clothing's are designed to create a positive change in the body; for pregnant women's, patients with motor disability etc.

Bio-Sensing Clothing: Electric sensors integrated into clothing have given rise to this class of medical apparel. These skin-near garments are used to measure vital statistics like heart rate, body temperature, and pulse rate. These garments can also be found in tiny electrical gadgets like smart watches. Nowadays, research is focused on creating increasingly complex, yet smaller, textile-based objects that only cover a small portion of the body. These products fell under the category of smart devices.

Sport Functional (Sportech): These types of clothing are used to enhance the functionality of sports person and it is one of the fastest growing segments in the clothing industry. Due to increase aging population people are moving towards a healthy lifestyle that automatically crates a huge demand for sports clothing. The main properties a sport functional should include are temperature regulation, moisture management, stretch, odor reduction and light weight. The principal govern that should be kept in mind while design sport functional clothing is:

- Compression therapy to enhance blood flow via the muscles
- Using aerodynamics in high-speed sports to lessen wind and air drag

Class	Subclass	Description
Protective-functional (Protech)	- Protection against environmental hazard - Protection against biological, chemical and radiation hazard - Protection against Injury	Protection from severe temperatures, fire, rain, snow, dust, wind, and UV radiation. Protection from harmful chemicals, poisonous gases, bodily fluids, bacteria, and radioactive particulates when ingested, absorbed through the skin, or in contact with the skin Protection from slashes and cuts as well as blunt impact
Medical-functional (Meditech)	- Therapeutic and rehabilitative - Bio-sensing	Pressure shoes and clothing for managing scars and venous and lymphatic issues Monitoring of bodily functions, including heart rate, blood oxygenation, body temperature, and telemedicine applications

Sports-functional (Sportech)		Enhancing performance, reducing tiredness, and body sculpting to reduce drag
Vanity-functional		Body contouring, support, and shaping for better appearance
Cross-functional assemblies		Performance, safety, support for life, comfort, and communication with several functions
Clothing for special needs		Adaptive clothes for the elderly, young children, and disabled

Source:https://www.researchgate.net/publication/296845630_Functional_clothing-Definition_and_classification

Depending on the needs, these principles are applied singly or in combination. Sportswear offers safety while playing sports like golf, tennis, soccer, basketball, baseball, football, diving, and others.

As the technology developed, new classes of functional clothing will keep emerging in the field to meet the requirement of consumers.

Vanity Functional Clothing: This category of clothing is used to enhance the body aesthetics. As increase in large ageing population, a awareness towards health and body is also increasing and this helps in fulfilling the growth of this segment. Men and women with ageing bodies or less-than-ideal body types wear these clothes. It is a instant and ideal method of body-shaping without harming body. The primary purpose of this kind of clothing is body shaping, and the basic idea behind vanity clothes is to raise or compress specific body areas in order to produce a desired body form. These clothing is a combination of invisible support, padding, molding, wiring, required seams and construction. Examples of Vanity Functional Clothing includes Pants, bras and various undergarments that can life the sagging part of body and give a slim and flattening effect on the different body parts.

Cross-Functional Assemblies Clothing: This is a distinct class of protective cloth that simultaneously symbolizes many intricate capabilities. To create functionality across many classes, these textiles use a variety of materials, including metals, ceramics, membranes, polymers, and electronic textiles. This clothing system is the result of a combination of intramural and extramural projects that aim to provide more effective, lightweight, and comfortable clothing. An illustration of a cross-functional assembly Clothing includes military attire that offers defense against biological and chemical threats as well as ballistic injuries. These outfits are also suitable with various accessories like helmets, hand and foot gear that facilitate communication, and should be comfortable for prolonged periods of high activity and posture.

Clothing for Special Needs: The use of this category of practical clothes helps people with special needs live better lives. These include young children, newborns, breastfeeding moms, disabled people, paraplegics, etc. Some of these circumstances, such as infancy, pregnancy, and lactation, are transient, yet they nonetheless have severe requirements, just as individuals who have chronic illnesses. Each particular group has different needs from the others.

These clothes' designs can be altered to suit the wearer's needs. Most of these clothes are custom-made to the wearer's specifications to ensure comfort and satisfaction.

Conclusion

The functional clothing suggested above is not entirely unique because there will inevitably be overlaps in the needs and technology used, but consumption and demand for these clothes are rising steadily. This field develops and expands at a very high rate as new applications and products are created.

References

Clarke S B & O'Mahony M, (2007) Techno Textiles 2 Revolutionary Fabrics for Fashion and Design. New York, Thames & Hudson

Friedman, R.(2016). Smart Textiles for Designer: Inventing the Future of Fabrics. London: Laurence King Publishing Ltd

Koncar, V.2016.Smart Textile and their application.Woodhead Publishing Series in Textile: Number 178

Schneegass,S. and Amft,O. Smart Textiles: Fundamentals, Design and Interaction: Springer's International Publishing AG

Hu, J. 2006.Active Coating for Smart Textiles. Woodhead Publishing Series in Textile: Number 176

Websites

https://www.researchgate.net/publication/296845630_Functional_clothing-Definition_and_classification

https://www.textileblog.com/functional-clothing-buzzword-in-the-fashion-industry/

https://techuntermagazine.com/what-is-functional-clothing

https://www.sciencedirect.com/topics/engineering/functional-clothing

https://medium.com/@stitchdiary/functional-garments-when-garments-do-more-than-fashion-262d1ca7ef9f

https://sabukaru.online/articles/functional-clothing-lab-a-visionary-woman-a-visionary-lab

9. Environment Sustainability in Fashion Industry

Shyamli Pandey, Neha

Research Scholar, Student
Clothing & Textile, Department of Home Science
Bansthali Vidyapith

Abstract

The environmental and societal costs of fast fashion are amazing. It is clear that a change to sustainable fashion is required in spite of the reality that the harmful impacts of the fashion industry on pollution, water consumption, carbon emissions, human rights, and gender discrimination are growing. Increasing the moral treatment of workers while reducing textile waste and environmental degradation are the objective of the recent fashion ongoing trend referred to as sustainable fashion.

Although the fashion industry is growing, it receives more and more attention of the amazing variety of harmful environmental effects and the industry is responsible for that. Serious health issues are caused by the chemicals use in apparel production for both industry employees and customers. The pollution already has several other health consequences too. Fast fashion should be reconsidered in context of the industry's harmful impact i.e. environmental and social impacts, which also show the importance of more sustainable economic systems.

It is important to discuss current issues carried by the fashion and textile sectors and to educate people about them. Strong and powerful consumer demand has the ability to change the environment, society, and economies. In order to attain sustainability in the fashion sector, conscious consumption is necessary.

Introduction

The fashion industry is gradually being discussed and criticised in today's life. The concept of sustainable has known for so many years, the term "Sustainable in fashion industry" is relatively new, designers and producers first stepped out of the prototypes that defined the fashion industry in the early 1990s. The current fashion system i.e. known as "Fast fashion system" has affects on each and every human being on world. It causes environmental degradation, deteriorates human health and well-being and is crucial to both cultural and economic development.

According to Brooks 2015, "One main contributor to the wealth and poverty divisions in the world is fast fashion. While some people are following trends and upgrade their clothes multiple times throughout the year with new ones, others work hard for poor wages in the clothing industry."

"Cheap fashion is really far from that, it may be cheap in terms of the financial cost, but very expensive when it comes to the environment and the cost of human life. (Brown 2010 as cited in Comovita 2018.)"

Fast fashion is a process that goes against social principles. People who are born and lived in developing countries (such as those in Asia, Eastern Europe, Africa, and South America) frequently work long hours for low pay in severe conditions that pose a serious risk to their health and safety.

Sustainability in the Fashion Sector

Sustainability has grown into a concept of it and has become connected with ecological advocacy. According to Berfield (1987), The World Commission on Environmental Development defined sustainable development as "development that fulfills the needs of coming years without affecting the ability of future to satisfy their basic demands."

Sustainability is based on three major elements, which are: the environment and its protection, society and economy and economic growth. Thus, the US developed 17 Sustainable Development Goals (SDGs), which countries finally approved in 2015. By the year 2030, these 17 goals are expected to be completed globally (2030 Agenda). The SDGs' broad purpose is to give everyone on the world a more sustainable and better future (UN 2019).

Fig. 9.1: Sustainable Development Goals (SDGs)

There are many different variations on sustainable fashion, as well as methods it may be developed more sustainable. These types are related to more eco friendly development that is both socially and ethically responsible. Moreover, sustainability in the fashion industry also refers to use as well as production. There were seven key strategies for sustainable consumption and productions were identified (by Green Strategy).

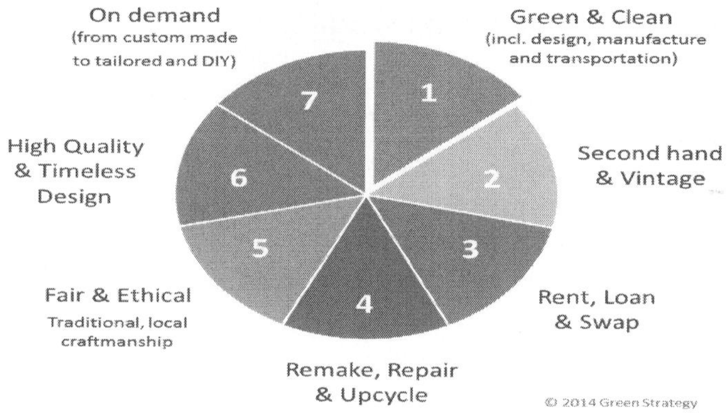

Fig.9.2: Seven forms of sustainable fashion

Sustainable and circular fashion is possible. If all seven forms merge together, it would be perfect and both sustainability and circularity will be observed within the fashion sector. In this way the garments will be produced in according to customer demands. These garments will be of high quality and high durability. They would be developed in such a manner i.e. not harmful to society and the environment. The 4th type of sustainable fashion includes repairing, altering and reusing clothing so that it can be used for a longer duration of time. When a person no longer prefers to wear a set of clothes, they find appropriate ways to dispose of it, (such as passing it on to a charity, a second – hand shop) so that the clothing can still be used by someone else. When a clothes cannot be repaired or reused (example, when it is completely damaged), it should be recycled so that the textile can be used again to create new clothing or other textile goods. (Green Strategy, 2019)

Sustainable fashion: Definition and Differences

Sustainability in fashion implies morals, adaptability, and product reuse. It is challenging to identify a single definition of sustainable fashion, because there are no common industry norms.

Cervellon et al., (2012), states that "The concept of sustainable fashion encompasses a variety of terms such as organic, green, fair trade, sustainable, slow, eco etc." According to Bin, (2014) "Each attempting to highlight or correct a variety of perceived wrongs in the fashion industry including animal cruelty, environmental damage and worker exploitation."

There must be a more detailed explanation of the areas of consuming, including as washing, maintenance, reusing and dumping, which can directly affect the sustainability of a garment (Cervellon et al., 2012).

Customer Demands for Sustainable Fashion

According to studies on consumer behavior, consumer's perceptions of ethics issue have been rising in the context of fashion consumption (Pederson et al, 2016).

Jagel et al. (2012) study is a rare example of motivation driven research into sustainable fashion (or even ethical consumption generally). They examine hypothetical and future purchases covering a range of 'sustainability' issues on consumers who self-report having performed at least one of the following: recycling clothing, boycotting a company and buying eco or fair trade clothing. They report a relatively high extent of ethical values such as social justice, equality and supporting the environment as support their hypothetical consumption behaviors.

McNeill et al (2015) conducted a survey "to explore 'fashion consumers' attitudes toward the use of sustainable fashion and recognize the effect of the 'fast fashion' on these attitudes. All participants in the study cited fashion and clothing as having a certain level of importance to them. However, where some participants noted that fashion was important ethically and stated that they believed all consumption should be meaningful, others felt that fashion's importance was centered on 'fitting in' and the social norms of fashion consumption".

The method which brands promote sustainability is also a problem. The use of phrases like "eco-fashion" or "fair trade fashion" in brand communication has increased significantly. Major selling elements of sustainable fashion in terms of attracting new customers focus around classic styles, original styles, long-lasting, natural materials, and stated health benefits. All of these selling elements may encourage buyers who are less ethical to purchase certain products. They appeal to consumers' selfish demands and enhance value, which would be reflected in the high costs.

Fashion's Environmental Impacts

After the oil sector, the fashion sector is the second highest polluter on earth. And as the sector grows, the environmental harm gets worse. There are many options and ways to reduce these issues. The first stage is to increase awareness and the ability to change.

Toxic compounds found in wastewater contain lead, mercury and arsenic, amongst others. Further, the contamination gets into the water, where it finally spreads throughout the world. The use of fertilizers for cotton production, which severely pollutes drainage water and evaporation fluids, is one of main source of water pollution.

The Fashion Industry's Water Pollution

Untreated harmful waste from textile manufactures is usually thrown into rivers in the bulk of places where clothing is manufactured.

How could we solve this?

Choose clothing from nations where factories must adhere to stronger environmental rules (EU, Canada, US...)

Use natural and organic fibers that don't require the chemicals use in their production.

Sustainable Clothing

Sustainable clothing is made of materials which are environmentally friendly, including recycled materials or fibre crops that are cultivated sustainably. In addition to upcycling and recycling clothing, going green often includes use of second-hand retail solutions. It also describes the process used to create these fabrics. Making clothes last by caring for them, mending and patching them, inheriting and using hand-me-downs within one extended family and community, buying clothing from thrift stores or any other stores that sell second-hand clothing, or donating used clothing to the stores mentioned for the above reuse or resale were all instances of historically acknowledged environment protection having a higher. With the present focus on sustainability and being sustainable clothing has progressed that included reducing the amount of clothing that is overproduced, destroyed, or disposed of in landfills as well as lowering the environmental impact of agrochemicals used to produce conventional textile crops (e.g. cotton).

Environmental constraints on sustainability (earth, life) Recycled clothes correspond to sustainability's "Three Legs of Sustainability": economics, environmental, and social equity. It also respects the "Three R's of the Eco system": reducc, rcusc, and recycle.

Giving rise to an additional area of economic gain is the use of recycled materials in the apparel industry. A new market for sustainable clothing will open up chances for more employment, a steady net flow of money into the world economy, and a decrease in the consumption of raw materials and virgin resources. Ultimately, lowering the sources of emissions, such as cutting back on the usage of virgin resources and raw materials, can cut down on carbon emissions from both the manufacturing and transportation processes as well as their associated resources and emissions. By utilizing what has previously been utilized, this also avoids the unsustainable use of removing materials from the Earth (i.e. recycling). Sustainable fashion provides a lot of advantages. Some of these include the fact that it uses less water, produces less harmful waste, releases fewer pesticides into the environment, and has superior quality.

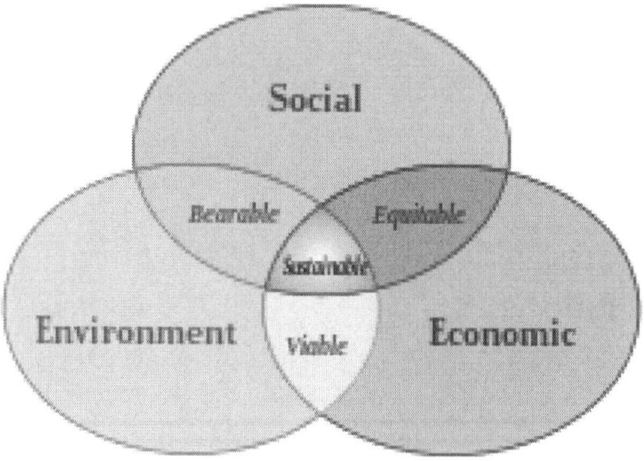

Fig. 9.3 The "three pillars" of sustainability bounded by the environment (earth, life)

Sustainable clothing has many benefits. Some being that it uses less water, it reduces toxic waste, it reduces the amount of pesticides released into the environment, and the quality is higher.

A Comparison of Fast and Slow Fashion

The current rapid fashion system and its opponent, slow fashion, should always be taken into consideration when evaluating the impact of consumer decisions on the future of the fashion and textile sectors.

Fast fashion is a concept used in the current era to describe the clothing brands that follow the most recent fashion trends and are produced at an unprecedented rate due to the influence of the internet technology, and industrialization. It refers to mass-manufactured, machine clothing i.e. of lower quality, less expensive and produced in large quantities. Inversely, slow fashion clothes are manufactured by hand, time taking in production and higher cost. Over many washes, slow fashion clothes are naturally cozy and comfortable. These may continue a lifetime or maybe many years. The use of organic recycled repurposed and up cycled fibers is important to sustainable fashion. The decision is determined by choosing materials with the least amount of chemicals, dyes, energy, resources, waste, and impact.

The need to convert a more sustainable fashion sector has been described by Kate Fletcher, author of Textiles and Sustainable Fashion. She came up with the term after the slow food movement, which had a major impact on the food sector. Slow Fashion is mainly defined by the fact i.e. not mass produced. The craft's man talents are also emphasized during the process.

Slow Fashion usually includes three steps:

- Design
- Production
- Consumption

Overall, slow fashion can be defined in the following way: "Slow fashion is a conscious effort to move away from the excessive consumerism encouraged by the fast fashion industry through changing consumer behavior and forcing the industry to embrace sustainability and to produce high-quality fashion. Unlike fast fashion, the primary focus of slow fashion is a continued commitment to creating fewer collections per calendar year with pieces made from high-quality materials that lengthen the life of the garment. Slow fashion is founded on the principles of conscious consumerism, environmental sustainability, and transparency, with design and production methods upholding high ethical standards." (Falkiewicz 2019)

DIFFERENCE BETWEEN FAST AND SLOW FASHION		
Category	**Fast fashion**	**Slow fashion**
Scope of the industry	Turnover $1.44 trillion dollars annually	Small business firms
Raw materials	Petroleum-based materials	Locally-sourced, bio-degradable, organic, natural dyes and natural materials. It also includes recycled, repurposed, upcycled materials.
Manufacturing	Cause environmental implications during production	It uses less harmful ingredients and employs eco-friendly traditional methods of production.
Protocols involved	Modern and unethical methods	Less harm to the environment as it involves conventional methods
Production	New styles every 2 week and more than 10 seasons in a year	Low volume, handmade, made-to-order and available in limited edition.
Presence of toxins	Large amount of carcinogens	Organic materials and safe eco-friendly materials for manufacturing.
Cost & quality	Cheap and low quality	Expensive and lasts long
Labour	Involves factory or workshop that employ workers at low wages, poor working condition and long working hours	Uses people from local or nearby area; serves as a means of providing livelihood
Morale/ethics	Poor working conditions, low standards in working place	Small industry with good profit and fair wages.
Sustainability	It is not possible to create eco-friendly product as it involves chemicals	Made in small quantity with high quality, with a motto to live with nature and not against it
Brands	H&M, Zara, C&A, Peacocks, Primark, Xcel Brands, and Topshop	Reformation, Amour Vert, Eileen Fisher, Alternative Apparel, Everlane, Re/done, Stella McCartney, Cuyana.

Conclusion

Nowadays, the fashion and textile sector are causing several issues for the environment and society due to, especially of the fast fashion sector. As customers become highly aware of the unethical work methods and damaging to the environment manufacturing processes used in the fast fashion industry, the demand for sustainable fashion is likely to increase sharply. The fashion sector can become more sustainable for the future by retarding consumption trends and manufacture. Principle "advices" for Sustainable fashion industry according to Green Strategy:

- If protection of the environment plays a major role during the processes within the world of fashion, sustainable development will be obtained;
- The Fashion industry should focus toward reducing and eliminating harmful manufacturing and usage;
- The environment should be preserved; the fashion industry must take precautions in order to not aggravate the problem.

It is clear, "that sustainable development and sustainable fashion industry is not possible without consumers` contribution to the development and their interest and involvement in sustainability issues." As it was said by Anna Lappé (an activist and a writer)

"Every time you spend money, you're casting a vote for the kind of world you want" (Anna Lappé as cited in Aburam 2017).

It was found that the fashion industry now has a huge harmful effect on both the environment and society. It implies that adjustments have to establish a sustainable future when such a sizeable and valuable industry creates trouble for both people and the environment.

References

Berfield, S. (2015). Making Ethical Chic. Bloomberg Businessweek, (4454), 56.

Bin, S. (2014). Sustainable Fashion Supply Chain: Lessons from H&M. Sustainability (2071-1050), 6(9), 6236. doi:10.3390/su6096236

Brooks, A. 2015. Clothing Poverty: The Hidden World of Fast Fashion and Second-Hand Clothes. London: Zed Books.

Cervellon, M., & Wernerfelt, A. (2012). Knowledge sharing among green fashion communities online Lessons for the sustainable supply chain. Journal Of Fashion Marketing & Management, 16(2), 176. doi:10.1108/13612021211222860

Comovita. 2018. 32 Thought-Provoking Quotes About Ethical, Sustainable and Fast Fashion. [accessed 9 June 2019].

Falkiewicz, M. 2019. Slow Fashion Guide: Everything You Need to Know. [accessed 24 October 2019]. New Dress Code.

Green Strategy. 2019. SEVEN FORMS OF SUSTAINABLE FASHION. [accessed 22 October 2019]. Green Strategy.

McNeill, L., & Moore, R. (2015). Sustainable fashion consumption and the fast fashion conundrum: fashionable consumers and attitudes to sustainability in clothing choice. International Journal Of Consumer Studies, 39(3), 212. doi:10.1111/ijcs.12169

Pedersen, E. G., Gwozdz, W., & Hvass, K. K. (2016). Exploring the relationship between business model innovation, corporate sustainability, and organisational values within the fashion industry. Journal Of Business Ethics, doi:10.1007/s10551-016-3044-7

United Nations. 2019. About the Sustainable Development Goals. [accessed 22 October 2019]. UN Sustainable Development Goals.

Websites

http://www.greenstrategy.se/sustainablefashion/seven-forms-of-sustainable-fashion/

https://comovita.eu/blogs/journal/32-thought-provoking-quotes-about-ethical-sustainable-and-fast-fashion

https://www.newdresscode.com/stylecode/slow-fashion#what-is-slow-fashion

https://www.un.org/sustainabledevelopment/sustainable-development-goals/

10. Natural Dyeing for Textiles

Shilpa Basavaraj

Designation: Independent author
(Alumni of NIFT New Delhi 1997-99 batch)

Abstract

There is historical evidence of natural dyes being used for textiles way back 5000 years ago, but since the modern era, the use of synthetic dyes has sidelined them. In 1856, a British chemist William H Perkin invented commercially viable synthetic dyes that made it much easier to use and had a wide range of vibrant colors, so the concept of natural dyes became endangered[1] . Great Britain was the first country to use synthetic dyes on textiles, so soon they realized the ill effects it has on the environment, people working in the industry and the ecosystem overall, this is when the technology was passed on to Asian countries.

Awareness about the harmful effects of synthetic dyes and their discharge on the environment has forced the textile industry to look at alternatives. Fashion designers are now exploring the value and limitations of natural dyes, and work around the limitations into unique selling propositions, first for their own understanding and then to make the consumer understand. This is the root level change required for the future of re-introduction of forgotten skill that needs revival, in the process it will help the people in the supply chain and the environment.

Introduction

The apparel and textile industry is as old as the human civilization, though the fashion has evolved through the ages. Until 1856, all the textile material was dyed using natural pigments that was available from the nature either from plants, minerals or animals. This was the golden era for the environment because what came from nature went back to nature. We humans are massively depleting all natural resources such as water, air and soil. If we do not correct our course, the nature will have its plan of corrective action and humans might not be part of that plan.

Textile industry is one of the top 10 most polluting industry globally. According to the Ellen MacArthur Foundation, textile production uses around 93 billion of water in the textile manufacturing process. It is high time that we need to find ubic

1 William H Perkin, Wikipedia

meters of water annually Vogue Magazine. March 2020 [1] .Colour dyeing consumes the maximum amount an alternative to synthetic dyeing, finishing and printing. This awareness need to be built in the minds of everyone in the complete supply chain right from fashion designers to the end users of fashion.

Fig. 10.1

Difference between different types of Dyes

Azo Dyes	Organic Dyes	Natural Dyes
Large class of organic compounds with nitrogen and carbon molecules that are commercially used as dyes[2]	A mixture of carbon-containing organic substances with pigments, which can be inorganic or organic substances[3]	Natural pigment extract from plants, minerals or animals. Most of the natural extracts are from plant sources that are regenerative
Extremely harmful for the people working in the industry that uses azo dyes	Since organic dyes are still synthetic dyes, there are negative influence on the health of people working	Since all the ingredients are natural, there is absolutely no negative impact on people's health. In-fact sometimes there might be some healing due to the use of some medicated herbs
Water after process becomes carcinogenic due to chemical compounds	Water after process contains toxins that can cause a lot of environmental issues	Water after process just contains natural ingredients that can act as a manure for crops
Soil that comes in contact with azo is damaged badly	Soil has a lot of negative impact if the discharge from these dyes are directly released without treating	Soil gets enriched with some of the herbs discharge and acts as an excellent manure
Air is polluted during the process of boiling these chemicals	Air gets polluted during the process of boiling these chemicals	No harm to the environment

1 Vogue Magazine. March 2020
2 Azo dye, Wikipedia
3 Organic Dye, Science Direct

What are Natural Dyes?

All natural pigments derived from the nature and are regenerative, when impregnated with water and certain types of fixer and softeners (which also are natural derivatives) without the use of any synthetic chemicals are considered natural dyes. At every stage of dyeing from scouring, bleaching, pretreatment, dyeing, fixing and softening all these processes use only natural ingredients either from different parts of plants, mud, insects or minerals.

There is a misconception in some individuals thought process that is "vegetable dyeing" this is not correct as vegetables are not the only ingredients in this process, though a few vegetables also may be used, there are a lot of other roots, leaves, flowers, rhizomes, bark, mud, insects and minerals together form the term natural dyeing

Types of Natural Dyes

1. There are three main types of natural dyes:
2. Plant dyes: dye extracts derived from various parts of plants
3. Animal/insect dyes: dye extracts derived from animal parts or whole insects
4. Mineral dyes: Dye extracts derived from natural minerals

Examples of Dye Yielding Plants, Animals or Minerals

Origin	Variety	Part used | colors derived
Plants	Pomegranate, Indigo, Madder, Marigold, Myrobalan, Acacia Catechu, Annatto	Leaves, bark, flowers, fruit, root, seed, etc | Blues, browns, yellow, orange , etc
Animals	Lac, Cochineal, sea snails,	Insects, shell, etc | lac gives bright red color
Minerals	Rock, earth, crust	chrome yellow, iron buff, Prussian blue, nankin yellow and manganese brown

Variants of Natural Dyeing

There are subtle aspects that make a major difference in the ingredients used for natural dyeing on textiles. There are certain dyeing units that use metal mordants like potash alum, ferrous sulphate or copper sulphate. These metal mordants are not harmful but have ill effects on the environment and the water cannot be used in farms as it is not suitable for crops.

There are a few natural dyeing units that are aware of the ill effects of the metal mordants and work completely with natural mordant's, wetting agents, fixers or softeners, this type of dyers are very few and can be found in industrial scale as well as artisanal scale. There are a few other natural dyers who are working towards dyeing textiles for healing purposes (for example, Ayurveda healing through textiles).

Dyeing with metal mordants	100% natural dyeing	100% natural dyes along with wellness herbs
A few metallic components are used as mordant's during dyeing process	All the raw material used for dyeing will be 100% natural	Along with the natural components some wellness herbs will be used to make it medicinal
The discharge from his will be harmful for the environment	There will not be any harm from the discharge of this	The discharge from this kind of dyeing bath may be beneficial for the farm land
Water after dyeing this cannot be used for farming purpose, there are possibilities of damage to the crop	Water used in this kind of dyeing can be used for farming purpose	Water from this kind of dyeing will be beneficial for the crop in the farm
People working in this kind of dyeing unit, may still be vulnerable to certain dangers in health	People working in this kind of dyeing unit will not have any danger to their health	People working in this kind of dyeing unit me have some health benefits

Formats of Natural Dyeing

Artisanal form: Since natural dyeing is an ancestral skill in the block printing segment of traditional textiles, there are artisans mainly in Rajasthan, Gujarat and Andhra Pradesh. A handful of these artisan families are still using the age old method of block printing and natural dyeing, which is a combination process. They use natural ingredients to pre-treat the fabric and use resist printing methods and also use natural pigments to print on fabrics, when they dye this in natural dye extracts produce amazing results.

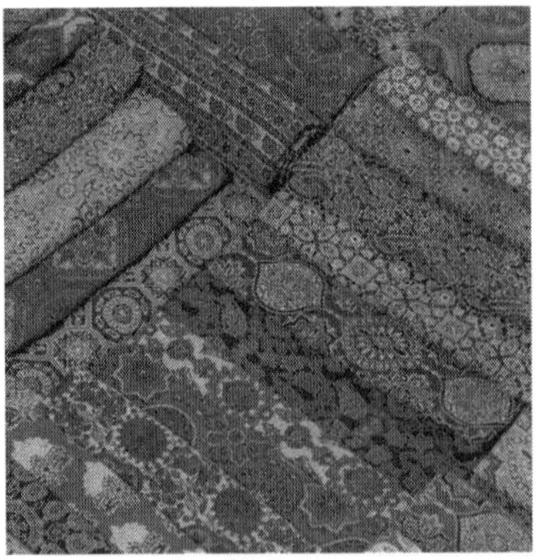

Fig. 10.2 Ajrakh block printing

Fig. 10.3 Bagru block printing

Fig.10.4 Sanganer block printing

Fig.10.5 Kalamkari block printing

NGOs and social enterprises form: There are some NGOs and social enterprises that have started natural dyeing in a small format without the use of machinery. This kind of dyeing is done in large vessels and cement tanks used for washing. They generally do yarn dyeing and fabric dyeing in small quantities that is feasible for individuals to handle.

Industrial form: In the past decade, some industries that have slowly started their research and development work on natural dyes. Such industrial units use machines for natural dyeing like in conventional synthetic dyeing units. These units dye fibre, yarn, fabric & garments.

Stages of Natural Dyeing in Textiles

Conventional synthetic dyeing can be done at different stages in textiles and the same applies to natural dyeing as well, though there are a few limitations in a certain type of natural dyeing.

Stage 1-Fibre dyeing (Stock or top dyeing): In this process the fibre is dyed even before it is sent for spinning of yarn. Loose fibres are loaded onto a fibre dyeing machine with dye bath at certain temperature and dyed. This kind of dyeing yields unevenly dyed fibre when converted into yarn and either knitted or woven will have a mélange like effect on the fabric (grainy affect).

The fibre dyeing is a suitable process for natural dyeing, but this has to be done in machines and there is a minimum order quantity required based on the machine capacity and spinning mills minimum requirement. So this is possible only at an industrial level.

Fig.10.6 Natural dyed fibre

Stage 2-Yarn Dyeing: In this process the fibre is spun into a yarn in its natural color and the yarn is dyed to the desired shade as hanks, which is widely used for yarn dyed stripes, jacquards, brocades, etc. This process can be done in a small format as well as in an industrial format.

Fig.10.7 Natural dyed yarn

Stage 3-Fabric Dyeing: There are different types of fabric dyeing processes such as small format artisanal form, jigger machine, winch machines, soft flow machines, etc. The small format artisanal dyeing with jigger machines have produced fairly good results, but in the soft flow machines, there have been streak marks and patches to overcome this research has been in progress. Natural dyeing has been done both on circular knitted fabrics as well as woven fabrics in different forms. This is one of the most widely used form of dyeing.

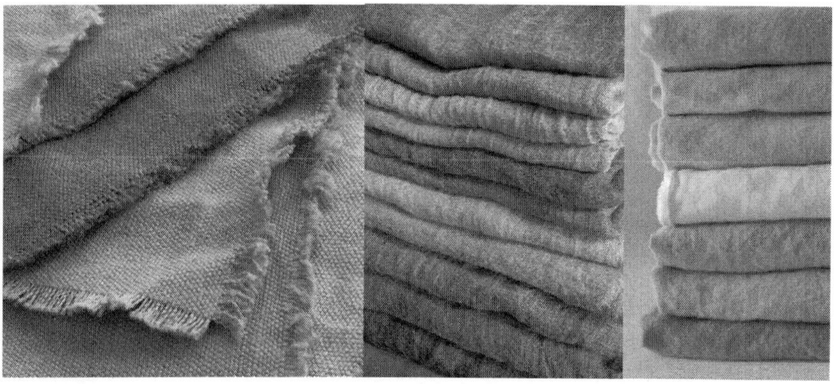

Fig.10.8 Dyed Fabric

Stage 4-Garment Dyeing: Dyeing can be done after the garment is sewn also and that has a very different look to the garment with a washed effect on the sleeve stitches, bottom hem like in denims. This kind of dyeing is usually done only in garment dyeing machines. These machines are called paddle dyers. Garments without any lining can be garment dyed. There are a lot of detailed work like the kind of thread used, kind of buttons and zippers used on the garment that needs to be considered for garment dyeing. T-shirts, shirts, leggings, pants , kids wear are some of the items that can be garment dyed.

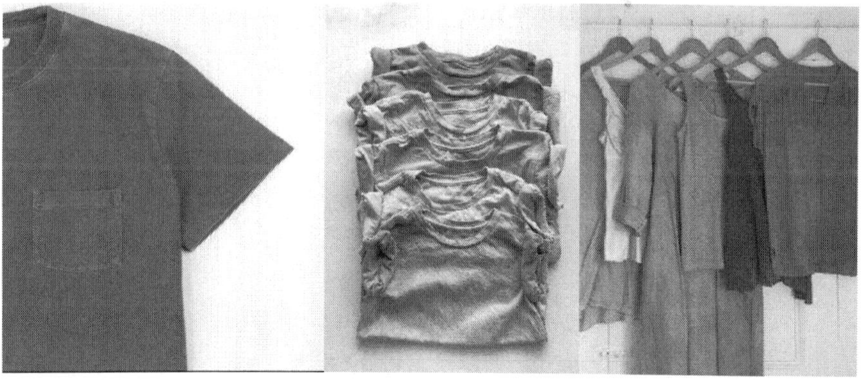

Fig.10.9 Dyed Garments

Stage 5-Special effects Dyeing: There are different kinds of effects that can be done on yarn, garments and fabrics, like the space dyeing, tie and dye, shibori, roller effect, sprayed effect, etc that gives a different look to the end product apart from all the dyeing forms mentioned above.

Fig.10.10 Space dyeing

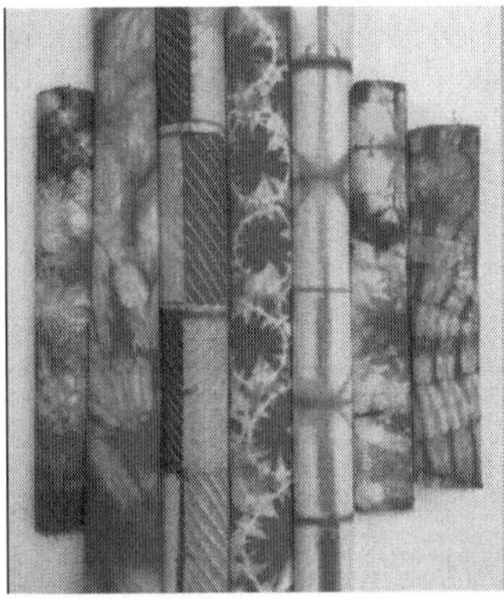

Fig.10.11 Shibori

Fig.10.12 Roller

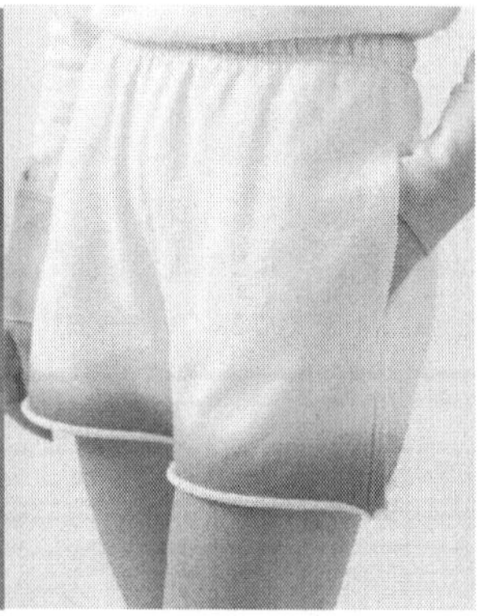

Fig.10.13 Spray

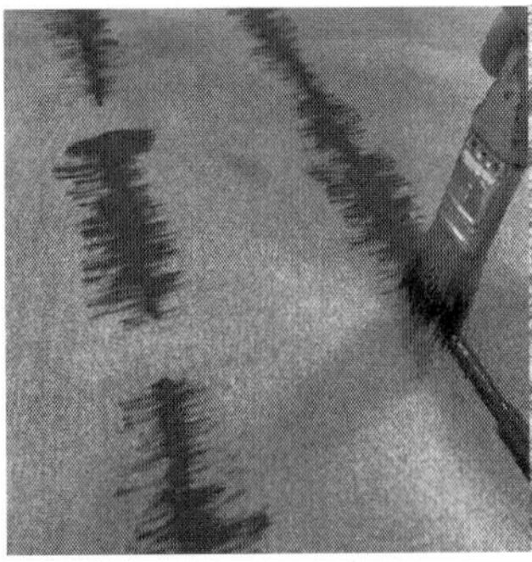

Fig.10.14 Painted effect

Fig.10.15 Dry brush stroke

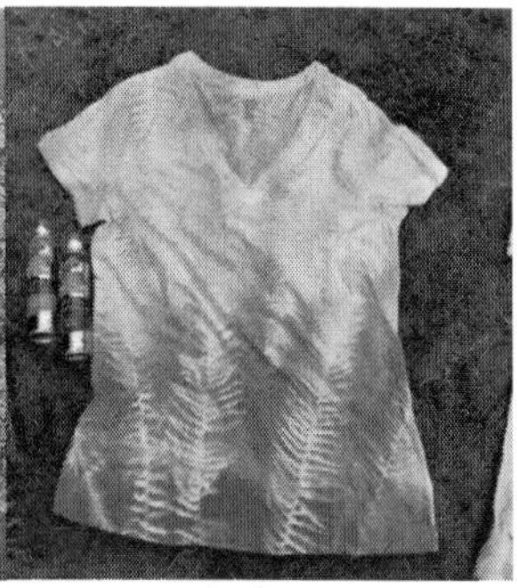

Fig.10.16 Spray effect

Process of Natural Dyeing

The process of natural dyeing is similar to the synthetic dyeing, but since it is natural raw materials used, some of these processes might take longer duration of time.

- **Scouring**: First process in dyeing is to clean the fibre / yarn / fabric. The raw material is contains dirt, wax or dust, which is further waxed during spinning or weaving. To ensure colour stability, all these impurities need to be removed from the surface of the fibre or yarn to enable even dyeing. If these impurities are not removed, the uptake of dye stuff will not happen properly and the dyes will not penetrate inside the fibre, which will lead to discoloration as well. A better scoured fibre or yarn will have a softer hand feel and uptake of dyes will happen evenly.
- **Pretreatment**: Natural fibres do not tend to absorb dye pigments directly so a pretreatment with a mordant is essential to make the fibers receptive to the coloring agent. The better pretreated fibre of yarn will have a better fastness of the colorant on the finished product.
- **Preparation of dye extract:** In the natural dyeing process, the dye powder or extract is not readily available unlike the synthetic dye stuff, which is available off the counter. In the past decade, a few companies that have got into natural dyeing extract, but this is still in a nascent stage and the authenticity of these extracts and other auxiliary items available off the counter are not proven. Further, the cost of these readily available dye stuff is extremely high, so not many dyeing companies are venturing into this yet.

The preparation of the dye stuff can be done in four different ways:

a. Raw material is used in its original form like full leaves or flowers - though the complete essence of the dye might not be absorbed in the dye bath in this method.

b. Pulverized extract from the natural dried ingredient either from plant, animal or mineral need to be boiled to make a decoction.

c. Soxhlet extraction- this is in experimental stage in the textile industry still and the requirement for chemical alcohol is a concern in this type of extraction.

d. Nano particles in the use of textile dyeing – This technology is very new and still in the research stage.

e. At present, the 1st and 2nd methods of dye preparation are widely used in the natural dyeing industry.

- **Dyeing:** A dye bath is prepared with the liquor water ratio required at a certain temperature based on plant fibre of protein fibre that is being dyed. After the dyeing process is completed the yarn or fabric or garment is washed thoroughly to ensure any excess dye particle settled in the fibre /yarn /fabric.

- **Testing**: The dyed fabric is better to be tested for some basic parameters of light fastness, color fastness and rubbing fastness, the global standards for this would be between 3-4 and above that.
- **Labelling**: The end product labelling on the content and wash instructions should be very clear based on the test results, that way the customer who is purchasing the product is well aware of it.

Standardization of Natural Dyes

The natural dye stuff extract standardization is yet to be achieved unlike the synthetic dyes. Though a natural ingredient may be derived from the same tree or plant the color after dyeing in different baths will vary and an exact matching of color is almost impossible to achieve currently. I would like to illustrate this point with an example for better understanding:

Parameters for sourcing the turmeric dye extract used on cotton yarn:

- Place where the turmeric is grown
- Temperature of that place
- Season in which the turmeric is sown
- Rainfall in the region
- Where is the plant seedling from
- Any pest attack on the crop
- Time of harvest
- Quality of soil during the crop
- Companion crops planted along with turmeric
- Carbon content in the soil
- Neighboring land what crop has been planted

Even when turmeric is purchased from the same land, the second crop will surely have variation either due to the crop itself or a various other factors such as:

- Water with which the dyeing is done
- PH level in the water
- Type of cotton used and from which region the cotton is procured
- From which region the mordant has been procured

- Temperature at which the dyeing is happening
- Season in which the dyeing is done
- Water liquor ratio

So, achieving the same shade repeatedly is a huge challenge with the current methods of natural dyeing.

Certifying Agencies

The concept of natural dyeing is fairly new in the industry and there are very few certifying agencies that can authenticate natural dyeing. There are many more auditing and certifying agencies, but currently none have anything specifically for natural dyes. A few of these certifying agencies are listed below:

Organization	Certificate
OEKO-TEX (Germany)	A certifying agency keeping a tab on the use of harmful chemicals. They do not have anything specific to identify natural dyeing
Bluesign (Switzerland)	A company that will walk with the partner company to comply with sustainability in the processes and not just audit and point on the corrective actions. Again not specific to natural dyeing
Global Organic Textile Standard (GOTS)	Standards set by a collaboration between companies in Germany, Japan, the US, & UK. Control over the use of hazardous chemicals and promotion of use of safety equipment in the industry. Certifying agency has nothing specific for natural dyes
IVN (Germany)	Certifying agency for organic fashion. Nothing specific for natural dyes
ZDHC (Holland)	Mainly for the hazardous discharge from the chemical dyeing textile industry to keep a check. They need to certify that the discharge from the natural dyeing plants are absolutely harmless

Testing Agencies

There are a lot of textile testing laboratories internationally as well as in India that test on all required parameters for synthetically dyed and treated textiles[1]. In the recent past, Intertek has come up with a new section called the "Vegan mark verification program", which can check for traces of animal derived material present in textiles. They also have ToxClear, which is an innovative digital chemical management platform for fashion industry stakeholders to detox their supply chains by reducing hazardous chemicals used in the input, process, and output stages.

Eurofin is another testing lab that does vegan verification, but does not have any testing parameters set for natural dyes. Synthetic dyes testing process will be totally different as the chemicals they will be using is to check parameters of synthetic dye

1 NABL list of labs for testing of textiles

stuff, when natural dye stuff is used, there is a requirement to create a whole new system to check those parameters . Testing labs need to work on research related to natural dye stuff.

Advantages of Natural Dyes

There are a lot of advantages of natural dyes, to mention a few:

- Renewable and regenerative raw materials
- Has positive health effects on consumers who use it
- No harm from discharge from natural dyeing that can be used as manure for farming
- Require huge quantities of crop cultivated which would be a boon to farmers
- Extraction need a lot of workers to collect and process, so livelihood is created
- Does not contaminate water sources in the earth, in turn the aquatic life does not suffer from dyeing

Limitations of Natural Dyes

Although natural dyes have been used from centuries, it was forgotten to a great extent till just a decade ago, so there are many limitations

- More quantity of dye material is required for dyeing compared to synthetic dyes
- There is no standardization of dye material
- It is not available off the counter
- Limited number of colors are possible to dye compared to synthetic dyes
- Raw material availability is different in different regions
- The process of natural dyeing is lot more tedious and there has not been an exact formula that can be used
- Cost of natural dyeing is more expensive than synthetic dyes
- Awareness regarding natural dyes is way too limited still among the stake holders

One of the major limitations for companies or social enterprises looking to start a natural dyeing plant is restrictions placed on effluents. There is a lack of awareness on the subject among government officials at the Pollution Control

Board (PCB), for whom the word 'dyeing' is directly related to toxic chemicals[1]. They are not aware there are alternatives to chemical dyeing and processing, which do not cause any damage to the environment, or to the people in the supply chain. A very urgent need is required for the PCB to work on a parallel audit methodology for natural dyeing units.

Government need to understand the importance of natural dyeing to restore the environment for the future generation and to detox the earth, and have policies and subsidies for companies who want to start natural dyeing.

Conclusion

The stake holders in the natural dyeing industry are brands, consumers, fashion designers, supply chain manufacturers, farmers, etc. An awareness need to be created among the stake holders regarding natural dyeing and the benefits it has from creating a cleaner environment, better living condition for people in the supply chain, better value for the customers using it. Some of the limitations in natural dyes need to be converted in to special USP (unique selling propositions) like the same color cannot be replicated, which the fashion designers need to work on and pass this message in a fashionable manner to the customers.

Customers also need to reduce their consumption of low-priced fast fashion items and move to slow fashion natural dyed clothing. This is the shift is need of the hour. By shifting to natural dyeing, a lot more livelihoods can be created from the crop cultivation, dye stuff collection, drying of raw material, pulverization and dyeing which will change the lives of many any people. The textile industry is one of the most polluting industries, for this to change this shift from synthetic dyes to natural dyes is the key strategy.

References

William H Perkin, Wikipedia (https://en.wikipedia.org/wiki/William_Henry_Perkin)

The fashion industry is using up too much water — here's how you can reduce your H2O footprint. Vogue Magazine. March 2020 (https://www.vogue.in/fashion/content/the-fashion-industry-is-using-up-too-much-water-heres-how-you-can-reduce-your-h2o-footprint)

Azo dye, Wikipedia (https://en.wikipedia.org/wiki/Azo_dye)

1 Pollution Control Board's norms on colour dyeing

Organic Dye, Science Direct (https://www.sciencedirect.com/topics/engineering/organic-dye)

NABL List of Labs for testing of Textiles (https://nabl-india.org/wp-content/uploads/2020/05/List-of-Labs-for-testing-of-Textile.pdf)

Intertek's Vegan mark verification program (https://www.intertek.com/textiles-apparel/vegan-mark/)

Pollution Control Board's norms on colour dyeing (https://cpcb.nic.in/uploads/Latest_Final_Directions.pdf)

11. Artificial Intelligence evolution in Textile Industry

Shilpi Yadav

Assistant Professor
VIFT, Vidya Knowledge Park, India

Abstract

Artificial Intelligence based on basic physics with computer application based algorithm

Innovations and advancements made our life comfortable. The ultimate goal is to obtain right balance with calculative experience.

The global apparel market predict to increase from $1.5trillion by 2020 to approx $2.25trillionby 2025.

Young engineers have connected basic structure or polymers structure of textile material and developed several techniques in order to complete the whole process with ease in less than marked time.

As we consider the data of 1980's AI had been the part of major textile testing process.

With the boom of artificial intelligence and machine learning, textile industry also improvises their process of testing and quality control by using these two tools.

Assistance of AI improved industrial efficiency not only machinery but operational as well.

AI & machine learning in textile industry is in infant stage only and still it made remarkably mind blowing changes in the industry.

Research Background

As per M Shahbandeh study in Statista , the global garment market predict to increase from $1.5trillion by 2020 to approx $2.25trillion by 2025, the study conclude the increasing in demands of apparels.

Increased demands in the market will also increased the labor work with increased request of quality products.

In the scenario automation and AI enters with the intelligence of generating good quality product in order to match the increased demands within the time period.

By using these two tools textile industry reduce labor cost and manufacturing cost and meet the customer demands.

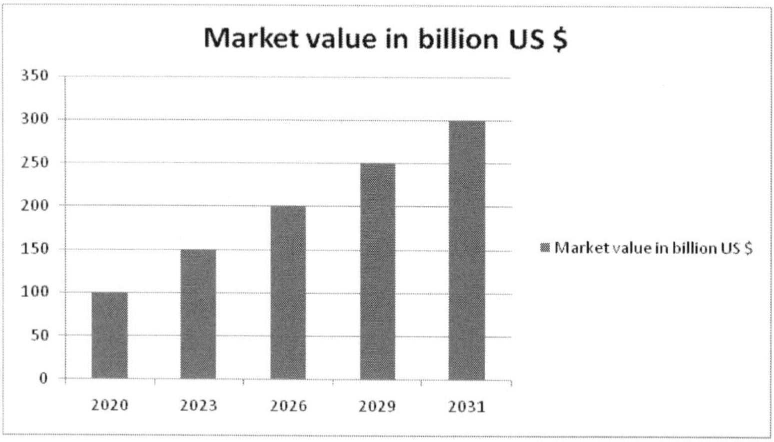

Fig. 11.1

According to the statistical data Luxury textile market worldwide from 2020-2031shows the growth of demand in the market for luxury category only.

AI technology anticipated to hit $62 billion by 2022.

The knowledge management part of AI is known as machine learning in this area machine uses data in order to perform task.

Demand of smart textile or smart fashion increases wearable technology increases.

As per recent market report market size of elegant textile is expected to reach USD 5.55 billion by 2025

Through implementing BLE (Blue-tooth low energy) smart textile can communicate with wearer through cloud data including biometric data such as blood pressure, heart rate, temperature and more.

AI re-routing the entire textile production process for textile manufacturers.

AI anticipates smart apparels or smart clothes which give leverage to IoT and electric sensors to provide better user experience. Smart cloth more provides more comfortable experience and more health focused experience. How fitness trackers helps the user to become more aware towards their lifestyle similarly AI with electronically sensors combination provides the same health benefit observation to the users. Smart clothing helps the physician in order to collect long tern data to identify or diagnosed the correct situation of the patient.

After covid-19 pandemic people become aware for health monitoring and emphases medical attention to their wearable products which is extending from smart watch to smart apparel.

"Who wants a fake Birkin bag" Anyone, especially somebody who spent at least $40,000 on the genuine article. Al can be employed in two different ways to assist prevent uncomfortable moments such as this.

AI is utilized by accounting behemoth Deloitte's One tool to detect design infringements. The program known as Dupe Killer uses data from millions of photos to discover tiny but unique design elements, such as an item's shape, colour, or even unique stitching patterns. This coverage in Vogue Business explains how Dupe Killer support brands in discovering and pursuing companies that are illegally using their own design trademarks.

AI is utilized by accounting behemoth Deloitte's One tool to detect design infringements. The program, called Dupe Killer, uses data from millions of photos to discover tiny but unique design elements, such as an item's shape, colour, or even unique stitching patterns. This article in Vogue Business explains how Dupe Killer helps brands in discovering and pursuing companies that are illegally using their design trademarks.

Literature Review

Artificial intelligence and machine learning improves the textile industries efficiency with quality. Fundamental concept of these two evolutions in technology based on real life challenges.

As per the Grand view research study shows the increasing demand of clothing in developing nation such as India, Mexico, China, Srilanka & Bangladesh and global textile market were expected to reach USD 961.5 billion by 2010 and are expected to show 4.3% by 2020 of CAGR up to 2027.

The evolution in the technology like Artificial intelligence, machine learning & IoT (internet of thing) has completely converted the textile business from labor intensive to technologically advance.

We can see the application of Artificial intelligence in almost every stage of textile industry from yarn manufacturing, inspection of fabric patterns, colour management, fabric grading, pattern making, supply chain management & merchandising.

Now we have more precise yarn prediction through computing spin, which reduced 62% of yarn grading mistakes.

It made the scaling of cloth's physical attributes easier and objectively classifies the textile comfort.

Fabric inspection gets easier by ANN technology (artificial neural network) which easily spots the weaving and knitting defects.

Data colour system used to maintain the colour management in all aspects whether its colour pigment or colour dyer etc.

CAD is used to make patterns, plot them on paper also cut the pattern, make markup planning and grading.

- AI tools are also used for managing transportation and packaging, also in warehouse management in order to maintain logistics and inventory.
- There are several AI application which industry implement now in their work process in order to achieve high quality results in short period of time such as:
- AI helps in fits approvals, company like Bodify ask customer for their photo in order to analyze the actual body shape and through machine learning data base generates the measurement chart according to the customer body type and size and made the desire style according to it. It reduces the fit problem and return process which affects the time and cost of the company.
- Company like Styleiser, also ask for customer photo and choose the product according to the skin type and colour of the customer again it helps to maintain the sustainability of the company by reducing the return rates.
- AI helps in deigning as providing different software's CAD projects which ultimately enhance the designing and provide different tools to reshape the whole process.
- Where should the textile industry adopt AI?
- Apparel Retails: The global trends in fashion are what drive e-commerce in the garment sector, namely. AI enables computers to recognize photographs and recommend online products that customers are more likely to purchase. Artificial intelligence skills enable e-commerce platforms to take advantage of information about customers, their preferences, and the similarities and variances in the products and services they look for. AI can actually produce a customized shopping experience in this way.
- Reinforcement Learning: The manufacture of clothing, in particular, involves a series of operations that are repeated. AI may be used to teach computers to take various actions based on the situational

conditions through reinforcement learning. In certain circumstances, it is best to make the best decisions that are possible. In this approach, Artificial intelligence applied to a variety of operations, including line balance, inspection choices, and cut-order planning.

- AI's natural language processing and learning skills can assist reduce the manual labor necessary for communication. It enables organizations to automate customer communications. AI can assist in commercial operations with little error potential and personalized customer interactions.
- Data analysis: The industry can benefit from artificial intelligence interventions that not only analyze massive amounts of data, but also forecast consumer trends, making major retailers error-free and better adapted to the requirements of the client.

AI's Effects on the Textile Industry

a. Trend-Seeing: With artificial intelligence, fashion firms may increase their revenue by quickly spotting emerging trends in clothing that would typically take days or even months to identify.

b. Machine-assisted designs: An AI tool could analyze and learn existing hidden images and then independently develop a completely new style.

c. Customer Experience: This covers everything from sending clients personalized advertisement notifications to notifying them when prices drop to answering their questions or resolving their questions with chat bots to acting as a personal shopper. AI can instantly propose outfits to customers, enabling fashion firms achieve their goal of improving customer satisfaction.

Where does IoT fit in now?

Internet of Things, often called as IoT, is one such exciting opportunity that has waltzed up the ramp of the fashion business. IoT is a technology that automates our world by enabling world wide web communication and interaction with commonplace objects like customers, suppliers, organizations, stores, etc.

You might be wondering how precisely this technology is affecting the fashion sector. IoT is now being used in more places than only cars, wearables, and smart homes, going beyond our wildest expectations. Did you realize that our wish for our misplaced clothing to signal their whereabouts may actually come true?

How is IoT Influencing Fashion?

Presently, IoT in fashion isn't just about the application of wearable's such as Google Glasses or smart watches, it also involves the stitching of invisible sensors onto cloth fabrics or enabling interconnected apparels to perform various functions such as notifying the user about the product's materials, assisting in detecting the product if its lost or even in facilitating style tips. We've reached the stage where technology and fashion can be combined to develop clothing that can be used to measure heart rate amidst workouts, where baby outfits can assess a baby's sleep pattern or even his/hers vital functions or where outfits can preserve our body skin from any pollution or decay.

"The Internet of Things basically streamlines the tasks for its users. It helps in cutting down the loss and in enabling more efficient management of inventory with the help of its tracking feature. From keeping track of any cases of fraud by barcodes and RFID tags, developing customer loyalty, and item popularity record to guaranteeing that one remains aware of present trends surrounding the customers. In essence, the Internet of Things simplifies the tasks for its consumers. With the use of its tracking capability, it aids in reducing loss and enables more effective inventory management. By using barcodes and RFID tags, one may keep track of any instances of fraud, establish client loyalty, track the popularity of particular products, and make sure they are up to date on current consumer-related trends. Some examples of businesses using IoT in the fashion sector include Coded Couture by IVYREVEL, a Swedish brand that collaborated with Google to create a Coded Couture app. This program is in charge of monitoring your activity so that clothing can be created. The app will provide suggestions for adding things like diamonds or a traditional style or a specific hue depending on where you go, whether it's a well-known nightclub or a renowned restaurant. Another example is FITBIT, which integrates its data into healthcare applications using Google's new Cloud Healthcare API. This gives customers a greater understanding of their own health while providing professionals with insightful data. Additionally, Fit bit collaborates with high-end clothing brands like Tory Burch (Fashion Meets Fitness).Another dated illustration was Amazon's Echo Look. This was a hands-free camera and style assistant with Alexa that provides a second opinion on the user's outfit via a style check. The platform's app allowed users to examine videos and images of their clothes, choose their favorites, group them into Collections, and share them with their friends. It also let users to find new brands and designs, as well as keep track of the colours they tend to wear. In 2020, the camera was abandoned".

Conclusion

In rapid change of fashion trends anticipating the upcoming trend it's a difficult task to meet also time consuming as well.

Through artificial intelligence analyzing the upcoming trend and according to that forecast start planning in order to meet the future demands by using various tools of technological advancement.

AI is made in a way to analyze the data qualitatively and quantitatively both which helps to analyze the future demands, analyzing the customer requirement and preferences, study the competition movements and predict the market trend.

It helps the fashion industry to reinforce their apparel sector in minutes or some days by regularly tracking the market trends.

Companies like Amazon built their AI program which study and conclude the fed images and generate the report whether the style is in trend or market acceptable or not. There are other big fat companies launched their own AI adventures entirely based on their own company work criteria.

AI is going to reshape the business growth and organic fashion in the textile industry in coming years.

References

https://www.statista.com/topics/5091/apparel-market-worldwide/#dossierKeyfigures

https://www.grandviewresearch.com/industry-analysis/textile-market#:~:text=The%20global%20textile%20market%20size,India%2C%20Mexico%2C%20and%20Bangladesh.

https://www.analyticssteps.com/blogs/ai-textile-industry-applications-and-impact

https://www.statista.com/forecasts/821415/value-of-the-global-apparel-market

https://www.statista.com/topics/5091/apparel-market-worldwide/#dossierContents__outerWrapper

12. Naturally Coloured Cotton An Ecofriendly Material For Fashion Industry

Dr. Vijeta Bhatore

Guest Lecturer
Department of Fashion Technology
Government Women's Polytechnic College Indore (M.P.) 452012

Abstract

Fashion Design is a fast-growing industry in today's world. Fashion designers need to provide comfortable but at the same time fashionable clothing to their customers. Fashion designing is basically designing clothing, apparels and accessories for a client based on his/her age; social, cultural and economical background; climate; gender and the latest prevailing trends. For doing this a fashion designer has to have a thorough knowledge of fabrics. There are a number of fabrics available in the market for designing and making of apparels. The choice of material for designing any clothing depends on the current fashion, climatic conditions, age and budget of the client and the occasion of wearing that clothing. Amongst all the mentioned criteria of choosing a fabric the most important criteria is that the material should be eco-friendly and sustainable. Because it is the need of the hour that such material should be used which is not harmful to the environment. And so it is the basic duty of a fashion designer to opt for fabrics that are natural, eco-friendly and at the same time sustainable too. An eco-friendly material is naturally made causing minimum harm to the environment and also can be disposed of easily in the natural environment. This research talks about one such eco-friendly fiber that is naturally colored cotton. Further this research explores the advantages of naturally colored cotton over other artificially manufactured fibers and also its limitations. The study also talks about the problems fashion designers face in opting naturally colored cotton in their designs and how these problems can be solved to a certain extent. Basically, this research is done to boost the usage of an eco-friendly fabric in the ever-blooming fashion design industry.

Keywords – Fashion Design, naturally colored cotton, eco-friendly fiber, Sustainability, apparel, clothing.

Introduction

Many fibers are available in the fashion market in today's time. Few are natural fibers whereas a majority of them are synthetic fibers. Amongst the natural fibers available to the fashion industry a few are cotton, linen, jute, wool, etc. These natural fibers are sustainable and at the same time are ecofriendly too. Since the usage of fiber is too high in the fashion industry, the designers and manufacturers need to focus their designs based on such materials. This in turn would also help in saving the environment. The word eco-friendly means that it shouldn't harm the ecological system. Such materials can be naturally harnessed or manufactured using such techniques which cause zero or minimal harm to the eco system. These materials once discarded don't pose any hazardous harm to the environment that means they can be easily biodegradable. One such naturally available fiber that is colored in nature is naturally colored cotton. This research is focused on naturally colored cotton and the advantages it provides.

Fig.12.1

Naturally colored cotton is an eco-friendly fiber as it is grown naturally without any use of dyes or harmful chemicals. Also when dumped, this doesn't cause any serious harm to the surroundings and can be decomposed easily. Naturally colored cotton is a natural fiber grown naturally in some parts of America, Peru, Pakistan, India and Bangladesh. Naturally colored cotton originated about 5000 years ago in an American city Andes. This fiber has a lot more advantages over other available natural and synthetic fibers and so it needs more research and development and acceptance in the fashion industry.

Different Fibers used in Fashion Industry

The fashion market of this modern era is full of different options of fibers. Amongst them there exist natural as well as artificial fibers. Fabrics are made using these pure fibers or even with a blend of these fibers. The below flowchart 1.1 gives a broad classification of the various varieties of fibers which designers can use in their apparel designing.

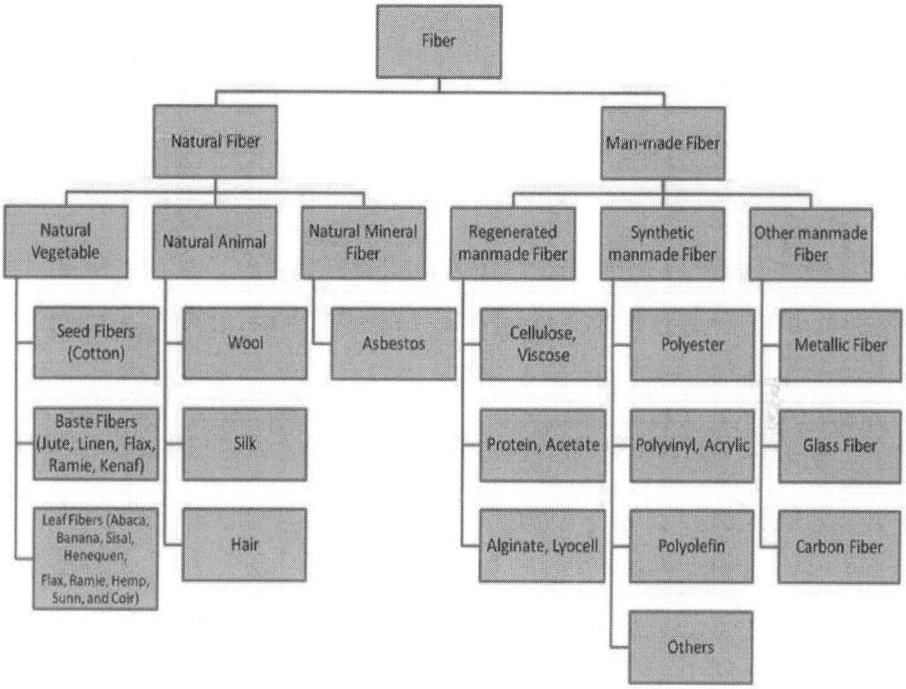

Chart 1

The brief classification of fibers is shown in above chart1. Naturally colored cotton falls in natural vegetable seed fiber, where it can be related to traditional white colored cotton.

Naturally Colored Cotton

It is a naturally grown plant product like cotton but in some ways, it is different from the traditional white colored cotton. It can be grown in a limited range of colors that include red, green and shades of brown. Naturally colored cotton comes has a natural chemical coating on it which makes the fiber fire and UV rays repellent. The plus point with this cotton is that it is softer than the normal white cotton; also its color doesn't fade on washing on the other hand the color gets darker with each wash. Yield of naturally colored cotton is less and it requires special harvesting techniques and so is not more popular amongst farmers. Naturally colored cotton is a natural fiber and so it is eco-friendly and causes no harm to the nature as compared to other artificially manufactured fabrics. Though it is an old fiber in the market still not much research and development is done on it as a product.

Fig. 12.2

History and Cultivation of Naturally Colored Cotton

Fig. 12.3

Naturally colored cotton originated in Andes in America around 5000 years back. Today the maximum yield of naturally colored cotton comes from South America. Mochica Indians of the northern coast of Peru are related with growing naturally colored cotton for the last two millenniums. Naturally colored cotton available in USA is of brown, green and white color. Whereas other parts of the world include hues like mocha, grey, black, tan, red, pink, mahogany, cream and blue. The natives of Peru are being encouraged by Native Cotton Project to grow naturally colored cotton as their skill of growing and spinning it was dying away. This motivation was given by the co-director of Native Cotton Project –James Vreeland, who discovered the pigmentation in cotton in 1970's. Ever since then Guatemala and

Colombia have evolved their own preservation techniques. These preservationist's organizations as well as individuals are growing gradually and are thus saving the myriad plant variety.

Fig. 12.4

Brown, khaki and red colored cotton were cultivated in large areas of Indian sub-continent and were commercially used to hand spin and weave for domestic use as well as for making novelty fabrics. The khaki, brown and red varieties of Cocanada1 and 2 were commercially grown in India back in 1940's and 1950's. Colored cotton grown in Andhra Pradesh was also exported to Japan. Assam cultivated khaki, brown, black and off-white colored cotton. Kumpta village of Karnataka grew G-herbaceum colored cotton of dull red color. Around 6000 varieties of cotton germplasm grown in India and elsewhere are preserved in National Cotton Gene Bank of Central Institute for Cotton Research, Nagpur, out of which 40 are of naturally colored cotton.

A major amount of naturally colored cotton is cultivated in South America because big brands like Patagonia, Espirit and Levi Strauss buy a bulk of this fiber which is colored naturally and there is no significant use of insecticides and pesticides. Sally Fox from University of California invented method of increasing the length of the fiber and then later Raymond Bird worked upon increasing the color palette of naturally colored cotton.

In the beginning of the 20th century varieties of colored cotton were released in Asiatic Cotton in India. Three varieties that are (a) Cocanada-1, (b) Cocanada-2 and (c) Red Northerns were commercially released in Andhra Pradesh. Due to the problems of low yield and bad fiber qualities the cultivation was discontinued for a while but the cultivation has gained momentum recently. This is as a result of the efforts done by Central Institute of Cotton Research, Nagpur and many other State Agricultural Universities who are constantly working on improving the fiber length and strength, maturity of fiber and also in the improved yield levels. These organizations are also working on different varieties and hybrids of colored cotton. Continuous efforts since 1990 has lead to the release of a commercially cultivated upland colored cotton variety named KC-94-2 from Jawaharlal Nehru Krishi Vishwa Vidhyalaya, Khandwa, in 1996. The color of the cotton depends on sunlight, soil nutrition and soil type.

The Advantages and Short Comings of Naturally Colored Cotton

Like every other fiber available in the market naturally colored cotton has its own advantages and short comings. Below discussed are a few such advantages and limitations of Naturally colored cotton.

Advantages

Fig. 12.5

- Naturally colored green cotton fiber possess excellent sun repellent properties as compared to other unbleached traditional white cotton. Traditional white cotton needs to be treated with various dyes and finishes to attain the same properties. The consumers who use naturally colored cotton get sun protection too.
- These cotton fibers don't need any extra fiber dye as they are dyed naturally. This saves a lot of water, energy and chemicals. Also the dying process which is avoided leads to less of air and water pollution.
- Since dying process is not needed, the time of manufacturing process is reduced.
- The color of these naturally colored cotton fibers doesn't fade with

repeated laundry or wash, but on the contrary, it gets even darker with each wash.

- Naturally colored cotton fiber falls out to be less costly as compared to the other artificially dyed white cotton.
- It is also flame retardant as the LOI (Limiting Oxygen Index) of colored cotton is higher than the traditional white cotton.

Limitations

- The fiber of naturally colored cotton is shorter in staple length, is weaker in fiber strength and also has low micronaire value. These drawbacks don't make it suitable for high speed spinning machines.
- The small size of fiber makes it strenuous to use it for manufacturing and processing of clothing.

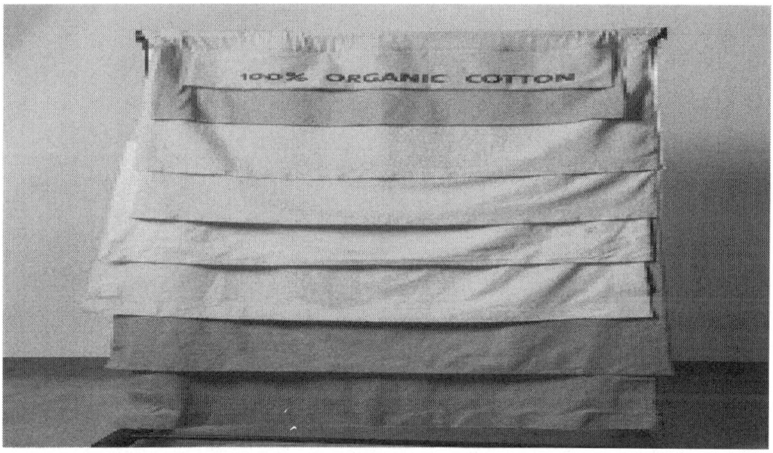

Fig 12.6

- Color of naturally colored cotton fades in direct sunlight if the crop is not harvested on time. The lint cotton balls on the field turn off-white or white if over exposed to sunlight.
- Naturally colored cotton comes in a limited color range and so can't be used in a variety of clothing or accessories.
- The yield potential of naturally colored cotton genotypes per acre is less as compared to other fibers. It is almost half as compared to traditional white cotton fiber.
- It fails to overcome the rapid turnover of the industries.
- Contamination of seeds is another big issue. The seeds of colored cotton can contaminate the seeds of white cotton and vice versa. That's

the reason why colored cotton fields should be restricted to small rural fields only.

- Lack of marketing is a bigger problem in the acceptance of naturally colored cotton in the fashion industry. Before increasing the cultivation, the fiber needs optimum marketing and advertising.

Major Indian organizations and Institutes working on–Naturally Colored Cotton-

- The University of Agricultural Sciences, Dharwad
- ICAR-Central Institute for Cotton Research, Nagpur
- SEWA- Self Employed Women's Association
- NITRA -Technical Campus

Various Uses of Naturally Colored Cotton in Fashion Industry-

- The fibers of naturally colored cotton have varied uses in fashion industry. A few of them are enlisted below.
- Men, Women and Children's Clothing- All types of attires like formal, party wear, casual, routine wear, uniform, lingerie, patient's dress, sportswear, and many such clothing can be designed and manufactured using naturally colored cotton.

Fig.12.7

- Accessories- Different accessories like bags, jewelry, hats and caps, foot wear, belts, eye wear, hair accessories, scarves, neck ties and bows and a few more accessories can be made using naturally colored cotton fiber.
- Home Furnishing- Home linens like tapestries and upholsteries, bed linen, table cloths and table runners, kitchen linens, bathroom linens, cushion covers, carpets and rugs, lightings and lamp shades, can be manufactured with the help of naturally colored cotton fiber.

- These fibers can also be used to make lace, tiebacks, tassels, embroidered furnishings, jacquard fabrics, power loom fabrics, duvets and quilts and also pleated window blinds.
- Some other uses- Diwali and festive decorations, handcrafted garments, gift articles, pet accessories, ribbons, toys, trophies, sports goods can also be designed and developed using naturally colored cotton fiber.

Need of Naturally Colored Cotton in the Fashion Industry-

Fig. 12.8

The fashion industry is fast changing. It keeps moving on as per the change in trends, season and occasion. This leads to a huge amount of waste, waste of raw material as well as waste of finished products. The dumping and disposal of this waste is a huge problem for the environment. For this designers need to opt for more naturally fibers that are sustainable and eco friendly. These natural fibers thus can be disposed off easily without causing any serious harm to the environment.

Naturally colored cotton is a natural fiber that is eco friendly and sustainable too. As it is colored naturally it doesn't require any chemical dyes for coloring it. This saves on a lot of time, energy and water which could otherwise have been used to color the white cotton. These qualities of naturally colored cotton prove to be healthy for the environment.

Another plus point with naturally colored cotton is its color doesn't fade with wash on the contrary it gets darker. So the fiber along with its original color lasts longer as compared to other artificially dyed fibers. It naturally inherits UV rays and fire repellent chemicals and so no extra artificial chemical needs to be done over it. The fibers of naturally colored cotton can be blended easily with other synthetic as well as natural fibers. By doing so, naturally colored cotton can be rendered the desired color shade and strength. These are the reasons why naturally colored cotton should be incorporated in the trending fashion industry.

Expert's opinion and Suggestions on Naturally Colored Cotton

As naturally colored cotton is an eco-friendly fiber, more and more fashion designers should opt it for their projects as a better and sustainable alternative for clothing and accessories. A few experts of fashion design fraternity were consulted and were asked for suggestions regarding the problems naturally colored cotton is facing in gaining popularity.

Many of the fashion designers are till date not aware of the brighter side of naturally colored cotton and for this design organization, policy makers and government should organize regular seminars, workshops, talk shows, trade fairs, fashion shows and training session. This will help to increase the awareness of naturally colored cotton amongst the designers, consumers and fashion design aspirants.

Fig. 12.9

Another issue is that naturally colored cotton comes in a very limited color range and for this the experts had to say that it can be blended with different colored natural as well as synthetic fiber. This will increase the color palette of naturally colored cotton and also will give increased strength to the otherwise weak fiber. Research has shown that even a small amount as less as 10% of synthetic fiber can change the hue of naturally colored cotton also it suggested that the content of different synthetic fibers should not exceed 10%. Too much synthetic fiber content will spoil the eco-friendly character of colored cotton.

Fashion designers practicing in rural or remote areas are not aware of this fiber. For this design magazines and newspapers should come up and do large scale advertising of this eco-friendly fiber. Social media too can play very vital role in achieving this goal.

The upcoming generations of fashion designers are not well aware of the benefits the fibers of naturally colored cotton. To solve this problem, academicians have to redesign their syllabus every four to five years. Revised and updated syllabus will keep the students in track with the latest materials of the market. Students should be given a thorough knowledge of eco friendly and sustainable materials.

The other problem is that naturally colored cotton needs surface ornamentation for making it aesthetically appealing. A few surface ornamentations that can be done on naturally colored cotton are enlisted below.

- Embroidery
- Quilting
- Appliqué
- Patchwork
- Trimming (Fringe trim, Sewing trim)
- Lace-work (either custom made or tailor made)
- Piping (it can be made from either self-fabric, contrast fabric, or may be a simple cord.)
- Beads
- Batik
- Smocking
- Printing
- Buttons
- Zippers
- Buckles
- Grommets
- Sequins

Conclusion

Naturally colored cotton is an excellent alternative eco-friendly fiber that can be incorporated in the Fashion Industry as a fabric that remains cool during summers and hot during the winters. It is much durable and falls out to be much cheaper as it doesn't require any dying process. A few areas like increasing the fiber length do need some research and development. Also researchers need to work upon safe, viable and profitable cultivation of naturally colored cotton. Traditional white cotton fiber or some other synthetic fiber can be blended with naturally colored cotton to gain strength in the fiber for high-speed spinning machines. Also this mixing process of other yarns can be used to render different colors and shades to the naturally colored cotton. The limitations of naturally colored cotton are very less as compared to the advantages it renders. It is clearly seen that Fashion Designers are not much aware of the NCC fiber and so it's usage in the fashion industry is limited. Joint efforts of individuals and fashion design organizations have to be made to make naturally colored cotton more and more accepted by the design fraternity. Seminars, workshops and conferences should be regularly organized to increase the awareness of naturally colored cotton. Social media can play an important role in increasing the awareness of such an eco-friendly and sustainable fiber available in the market. Academic institutes should update their syllabus time to time so that the young designers can be taught about these eco-friendly materials in their academic years. Fibers like naturally colored cotton need a strong back up to mark their existence in the market and create an eco-friendly and sustainable environment for the future generations.

References

(PDF) Development of U.V. and flame-resistant fabric from natural colored cotton (researchgate.net)

(PDF) Development of various colors and shades in naturally colored cotton fabrics (researchgate.net)

(PDF) Naturally colored cotton (researchgate.net)

"Sally Fox, the Organic Cotton Queen." Living Crafts, Spring 2008.

Durham, Ann. "A Cotton-Picking Good Time or How I Discovered a Cotton Gin in My Kitchen." Spin-Off, Fall 2002.

Effect of scouring and laundering on functional properties of natural colour cotton fabric | Request PDF (researchgate.net)

Evaluation of fiber, yarn, and woven fabric properties of naturally colored and white Turkish organic cotton | Request PDF (researchgate.net)

Lester, Julius. To Be A Slave. New York: Scholastic, 1968.

Natural Colored Cotton - Bing images

Natural Colored Cotton - Bing images

Natural Colored Cotton - Bing images

Natural Colored Cotton - Bing images

Naturally colored Cotton - Bing images

Naturally Colored Cotton | Textile Study Center

Naturally Colored Organic Cotton and Naturally Colored Cotton Fiber Production: Is it a Sustainable Solution? | Request PDF (researchgate.net)

Naturally coloured cotton: Growing awareness (researchgate.net)

Naturally coloured cotton: Valuable gift for the future | Request PDF (researchgate.net)

Ordal, Leslie. "At Cotton Clouds." Spin-Off, Winter 2010.

Organically Colored Cotton - Bing images

Organically Colored Cotton - Bing images

Organically Colored Cotton - Bing images

Organically Colored Cotton - Bing images

Properties of the Naturally Colored Cottons - PandaSilk

Rhoades, Carol Huebscher. "Colored Cotton." Spin-Off, Summer 2008.

use of naturelly colored cotton in garments - Bing images

use of naturelly colored cotton in garments - Bing images

13. Protective Clothing: A brief discussion and General Requirements

Dr. Aligina Anvitha Sudheshna,
Ph.D. Department of Textiles and Apparel Designing,

Abstract

Protection is mandatory for the well-being of people in certain occupations where they might be exposed to hazards be it chemical fumes, hypothermia, etc. As technological advancements are bringing new surges to the fiber and fabric advancements, there is also an equal increment in the hazards exposure to the workers in several fields. This chapter is intended to discuss the various types of protective clothing and their need and the present trends in smart clothing which were imparted with the capacity to analyze and interact with the surrounding environment for better performance.

Keywords: Protective clothing, functional clothing, smart textiles, protection, safety

Introduction

Protective clothing/ textiles are worn by millions of workers routinely to protect themselves from environmental hazards, adverse weather, and several biological, thermal, and physical agents. In simpler terms, functional and protective garmentscan be defined as garments or fabrics that are used by consumers primarily for protection purposes or for the functional characteristics of the garment rather than for mere aesthetics or decorative purposes (Adams et al., 1994). Protective clothing is mainly used as a safety measure for individuals/ workers. Safety as defined by Helena Mäkinen, (2008)is the freedom from unacceptable risk of harm.

The late 20th century has seen an unprecedented increase in the emphasis on the protection of humans from basic everyday life hazards. The intensity and means to combat a range of hazards continue to grow and have reached a phase of severe complexity. One of the major consequences of this can be linked to the development and exploitation of new fibers, smart/ intelligent textiles, smart clothing systems, and new structures whose main aim is to provide maximum protection while maintaining comfort and well-being (Shishoo, 2002).

Considering the design development of protective clothing, the category of hazards or the conditions in which the wearer intends to use the clothing is one of the main considerations. Protection is required from various conditions such as chemical exposure, hot/ cold weather, fire, bullets, ballistic, etc. For a design to be successful one should always critically analyze the specific functional requirement and the components which are to be optimized for eliminating or minimizing the risk to the wearer. Designing these types of clothing requires various research and knowledge from varied fields such as nanotechnology, engineering of smart fabrics, special production techniques, etc. Along with these aspects, the developed clothing should adhere to the regulatory standards given by the governing bodies. From figure 1 we can observe how the skin and clothing layers interact with the surrounding environment in air and water (Song et al., 2014)

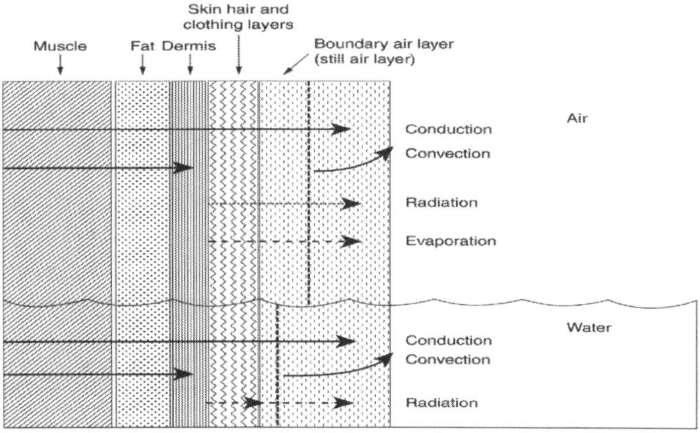

Fig.13.1 Heat and moisture transfer mechanism from the skin to the environment under air and water

The global market for protective clothing is sized at a value of 12.48 billion dollars during the year 2019, and the forecast trends suggest that the market is expected to reach 34.31 billion dollars by the year 2027 raising upto 14% CAGR (Protective Clothing Market Size, Share | Global Industry Report, 2027, n.d.).

Clothing Layers

Despite the type of hazard or environmental condition, a clothing item consists of at least one or all of the following layers as a part of the clothing item.

1. Outer Shell Layer

An outer shell is a layer that is in direct contact with the environment which suggests that it should be waterproof to keep the wearer dry, breathable, and sealed seams. In the case of gloves/ sleeves, velcro closure is the most accepted and the gloves were desirable with an added support for grip.

2. Inner/ Base Layer

The inner layer can be termed as the thermally insulating layer with high comfort to the wearer along with high-performing insulation materials. The inner material should accommodate several anatomical variations whilst providing comfort to the wearer.

3. Mid Layer

The middle layer provides additional insulation to the wearer. This layer tends to be loosely fitted compared to the inner layer. The mid-layer acts as an extended barrier to protect the wearer from external influences.

In general notion layering is the most focused on functional and protective clothing but, a complete clothing system represents boots/ footwear, gloves, headgear, and the insulated layers of the clothing. Apart from the basic understanding, there are varied areas in which protective clothing is required, some of them are elaborated on below for a brief understanding:

Thermal Protective Clothing

Thermal protective clothing is used to protect the wearer from radiative heat, sparks, heat, flame, drops of molten metal, etc. One of the key concepts is to achieve high insulation with low compressibility. The main performance requirements are based on the tolerance of human tissue against burn injuries. Several flame retardant materials were developed during the last few decades such as aramid, PBI, carbon fibers, PCM (phase change material), and mineral fibers just to mention a few. But recent advancements have been towards the thermophysiological aspects of the wearer, which suggests ways to get rid of the swear and excessive body heat without compromising the protective demands against external heat (Rossi, 2014).

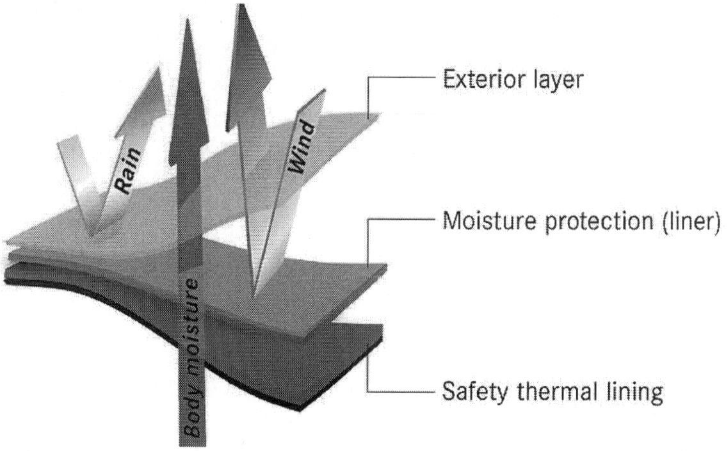

Fig.13.2 Fabric layer representation of rain and wind penetration

Chemical Protective Clothing

With the advancements in modern technologies, there is a multi-fold increase in the type of chemicals workers is exposed to ranging from liquid sprays, gases petrochemicals, pharmaceuticals, electroplating industries, and agricultural fertilizers. One of the basic necessities for this type of clothing is that the clothes should be impermeable and resistant to chemicals creating a tight seal against toxic gases or should be able to filter the dangerous dust. There are four levels of CPC (chemical protective clothing) level 1 consists of fully encapsulated suits with self-contained breathing apparatus, which is to be worn when a high level of the skin, eye, and respiratory protection is needed. Level-2 is a chemical splash suit, with disposable chemical-resistant overalls along with breathing apparatus, which is to be worn when the highest respiratory protection is required with lesser skin protection. Level-3 is used for concentrated airborne substances, in an air purifying mask full or half cover is used including hooded chemical resistant clothing which is recommended for level-2. In level 4 minimum skin protection is required without any respirators but gloves, footwear covers, and overall covers are required to preclude splashes of any hazardous chemicals (Bhuiyan et al., 2019).

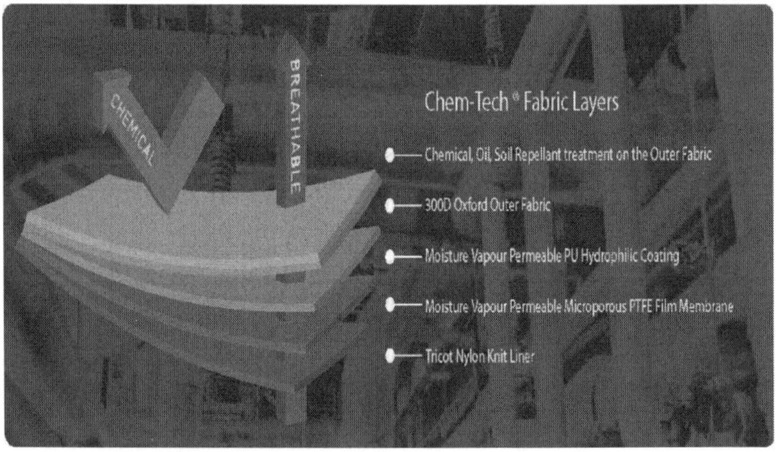

Fig.13.3 Fabric layer representation of chemical permeability

Cold Protective Clothing

In cold protective clothing, different types of cold environments such as wet, dry, and windy, etc. require a different type of final product and the insulation material is strongly affected by wind and body movements. The thermal insulation requisition for a specific environment can be predicted by using IREQ (insulation required) methods as per the IDO/TR-11079, 1993 standards. In this type of clothing, an additional layer of thermal underwear is commonly used as a part of the overall ensemble (H. Mäkinen & Jussila, 2014).

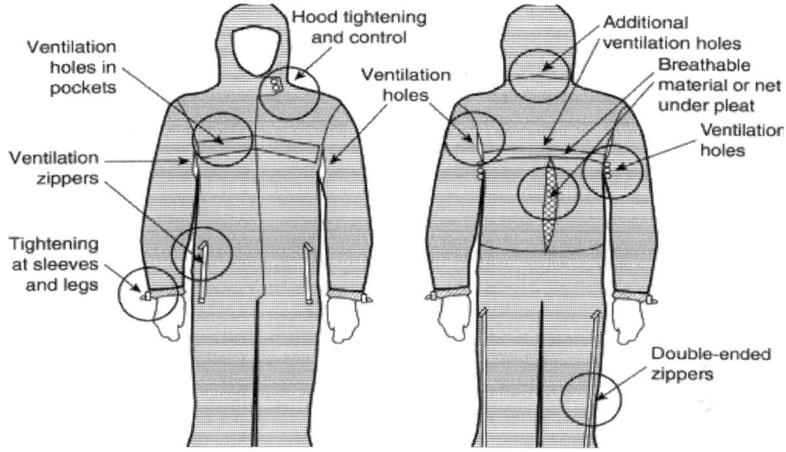

Fig.13.4 Design details with ventilation in the garment

High Visibility Warning Clothing

This type of clothing is necessary to signal the presence of the workers. Luminosity was imparted in order to produce an article of clothing with high visibility warning otherwise the workers can lose their lives due to mishaps. Some of the major parameters of the clothing include chromaticity, colour fastness to abrasion, washing, perspiration, and bleaching agents. Fluorescent yellow and fluorescence red-orange were considered to produce the highest visibility (Toma et al., 2000).

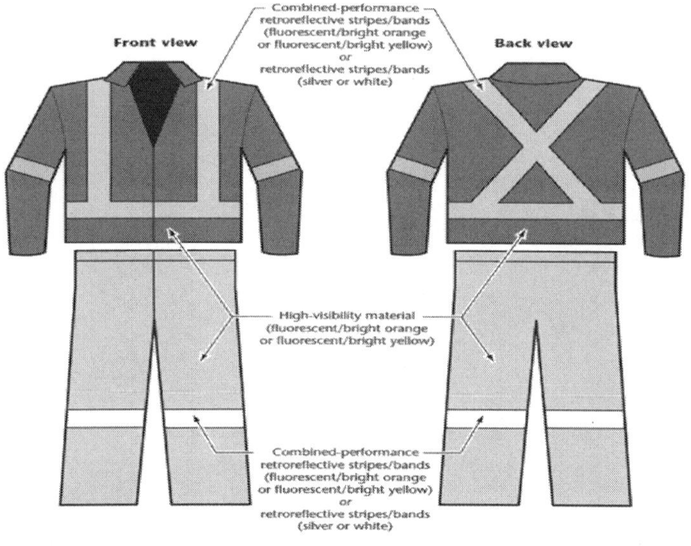

Fig.13.5 Garments for visibility warning clothing

Military Protective Clothing

Defense clothing is specially developed by the agencies of the armed forces. As military personnel works under a variety of work conditions some of the considerations are improved protection against the environment and natural threats during the battlefield. To survive in extreme conditions the clothing should maintain thermo-physiological comfort. As the protective clothing tends to be in layers all the layers or different components of the clothing should assemble together. Weight considerations are to be noted to ease off the excessive load carriage but the clothing should be most effective, durable, and recyclable with all the components having a multi-role. Some of the fibers available for this type of clothing are ballistic nylon, para aramids (kevlar, Taron, zylon), PBO (para phenylene polybenzobis oxazole), UHMPE (ultra-high modulus polyethylene), GSPE (gel spun poly-ethylene), etc.

Apart from ballistic properties, the apparel should also contain camouflage encompassing the ultraviolet, visible (0.4- 0.8 micron), near-infrared (0.8- 1.2 micron), and thermal far infrared (from 2.0- 5.6 microns to 8.0- 14.0 microns) to draft the surveillance systems (Carr & Lewis, 2014).

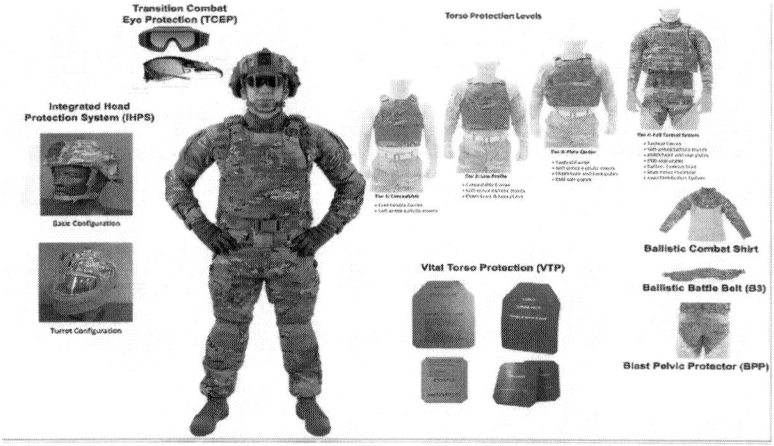

Fig.13.6 Different parts of the military and ballistic protection clothing

Medical Protective Clothing

Medical protective clothing should be resistant to biological contents such as germs, viruses, fungi, bacteria, and body fluids. All possible aerosol loads are to be taken into consideration to lower or eradicate the risk of contamination. Specific paths such as oral, dermal, and respiratory paths uptake should be determined to calculate the overall exposure when assessing any relevant toxicological limit values (Karim et al., 2020)"

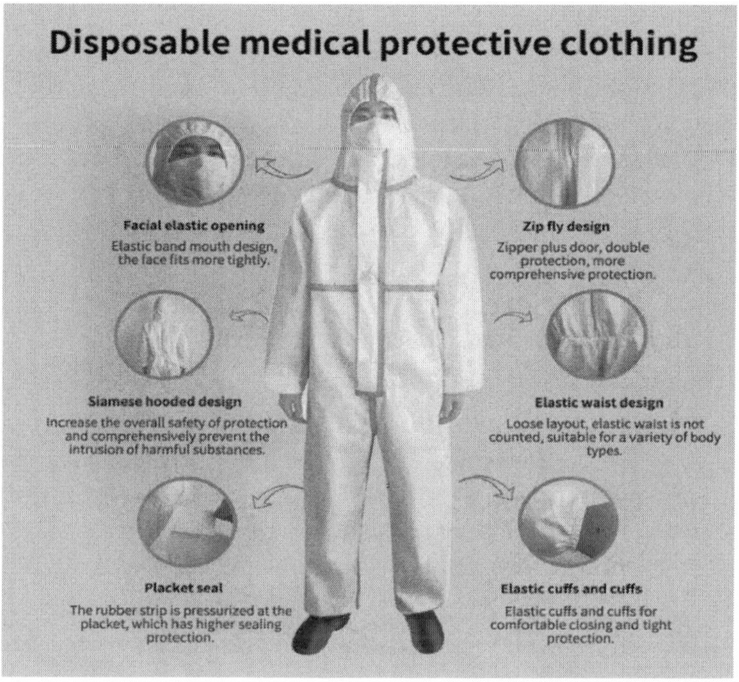

Fig.13.7 Personal protective equipment for medical protective clothing

Passenger Survival Suits

Fig.13.8 Survival suit for the underwater ejection

Considering the sea voyages and people engaged in several sea activities and the accidents caused in the sea have taken shape to form passenger survival suits. These are specially used for submarines where the ship is completely submerged in the sea and thus clothing such as life jackets pose a high risk of cold shock/ hypothermia rather than intent protective use. These suits will help to reduce water ingress and hypothermia even when the water temperature is below 5°C for two hours, and with the help of a life jacket which is to be worn above the suit, the subjects will stay afloat (Wissler, 2014).

Protective clothing against Multiple Hazards

Technological advancements have led to a phase where multiple specializations are required from a single type of clothing. For example, when an emergency team engages with hazardous materials encompassed in flames they should have protection against chemicals as well as fire. Thus duel events like these needs special reinforcements to provide the combination of protective clothing designs as well as materials for attributing appropriate levels of protection(Geršak & Marčič, 2013)

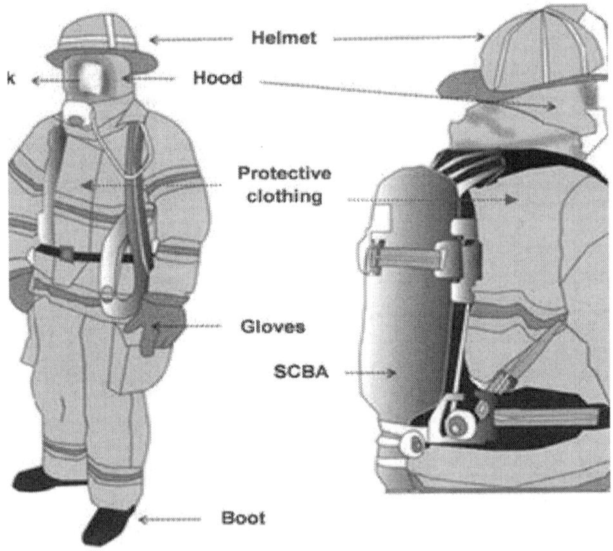

Fig.13.9 Basic clothing items for multiple hazard protection

Smart Textiles

The need for revolutionizing new materials which are intended to be useful in more areas rather than limited to a particular use was found to be in high demand (such as protective clothing for multiple hazards). Recent advancements pertaining to miniaturization of the electronics have provided a significant improvement in safety measures and health. Personal warning systems were embedded in the clothing systems with integration between the health, environmental sensors, LCD displays, vibrating elements, and much more. These devices were also named intelligent textile materials which can shield the wearer from unknown threats in terms of military textiles and firefighter's clothing where the outer layers automatically shield the wearer when there is a critical change in the external temperature without any hindrance to the movements (Dąbrowska et al., 2021)up to now there are not any requirements and standardized test methods enabling confirmation of safety of use and functionality of these systems in work environment. In the paper, an importance of evaluation of such smart wearable system in predicted utility conditions is highlighted. Three variants of the specially developed personal warning systems (PWSs).

Some examples include fabrics embedded with optical fibers, UV protective clothing, conductive clothing, etc. This type of smart protective clothing not only protects the wearer from external threats such as chemicals, flames, etc. but also can assess the internal capacity of the individual such as fatigue, heart strokes, acute diseases, and the physical condition of the wearer thus making the personnel aware of their status, thus rendering a particular task successful by providing medication at the critical times when necessary reducing the risk at several levels (Applications of Smart Textiles for Protective Purposes - Textile Learner, n.d.).

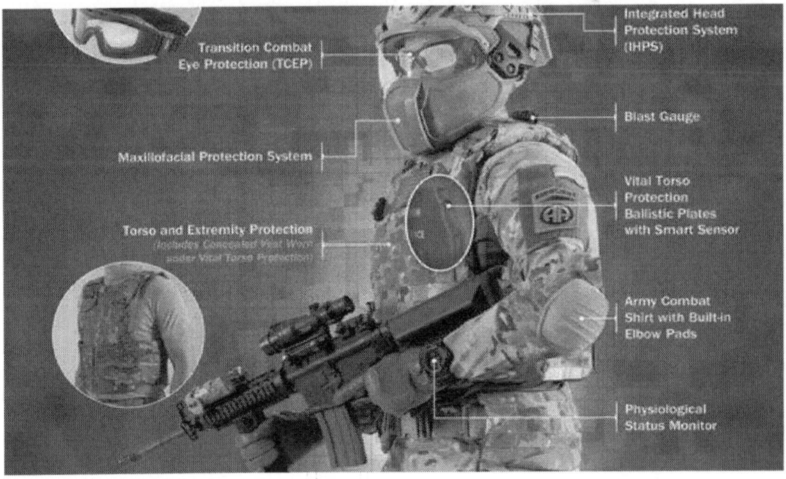

Fig.13.10 depicts the application of smart textiles in military

Each and every aspect is interlinked with the environment. New advancements were also directed towards cleaner production and recycling steps where ever possible to reduce the negative environmental impacts. One of the major concerns is the finishes imparted on the protective clothing such as antimicrobial, water repellant, soil repellent, etc. which have a tough time in terms of biodegradation.

Incineration is the most opted choice for medical textiles whereas most of them tend to have a recycling capacity. Therefore it is expected that the new trends will bring out positive change towards the end of cycle garments ultimately engaging in a closed loop of production and end of garment cycles.

Conclusion

Trends and technological advancements suggest that there will be an increased demand for the market. Increasing awareness towards environmental safety standards as well as personal safety with added layers of comfort and protection are leading to advancements in the materials, fibers, coatings, and blends development. In the process of designing relationships with technology, the user, and environment are interlinked to provide the best end results. The test methods employed were also incorporating real test subjects during the physical activity for the best results.

References

Adams, P. S., Keyserling, W. M., & Slocum, A. C. (1994). A Model for Protective Clothing Effects on Performance. International Journal of Clothing Science and Technology, 6(4), 6–16. https://doi.org/10.1108/09556229410054495

Applications of Smart Textiles for Protective Purposes - Textile Learner. (n.d.). Retrieved January 8, 2023, from https://textilelearner.net/applications-of-smart-textiles-for-protective-purposes/

Bhuiyan, M. A. R., Wang, L., Shaid, A., Shanks, R. A., & Ding, J. (2019). Advances and applications of chemical protective clothing system. Journal of Industrial Textiles, 49(1), 97–138. https://doi.org/10.1177/1528083718779426

Carr, D., & Lewis, E. A. (2014). Ballistic-protective clothing and body armour. In Protective Clothing: Managing Thermal Stress. Woodhead Publishing Limited. https://doi.org/10.1533/9781782420408.1.146

Dąbrowska, A., Bartkowiak, G., & Kotas, R. (2021). Evaluation of functionality of warning system in smart protective clothing for firefighters. Sensors, 21(5), 1–14. https://doi.org/10.3390/s21051767

Geršak, J., & Marčič, M. (2013). The complex design concept for functional protective clothing. Journal for Textile and Clothing Technology, 62, 38–44. https://hrcak.srce.hr/142613

Karim, N., Afroj, S., Lloyd, K., Oaten, L. C., Andreeva, D. V., Carr, C., Farmery, A. D., Kim, I. D., & Novoselov, K. S. (2020). Sustainable personal protective clothing for healthcare applications: A review. ACS Nano, 14(10), 12313–12340. https://doi.org/10.1021/acsnano.0c05537

Mäkinen, H., & Jussila, K. (2014). Cold-protective clothing: Types, design and standards. In Protective Clothing: Managing Thermal Stress. Woodhead Publishing Limited. https://doi.org/10.1533/9781782420408.1.3

Mäkinen, Helena. (2008). Firefighters' protective clothing. Advances in Fire Retardant Materials, 467–491. https://doi.org/10.1533/9781845694701.3.467

Protective Clothing Market Size, Share | Global Industry Report, 2027. (n.d.). Retrieved January 8, 2023, from https://www.fortunebusinessinsights.com/protective-clothing-market-102707

Rossi, R. (2014). Clothing for protection against heat and flames. Protective Clothing: Managing Thermal Stress, 70–89. https://doi.org/10.1533/9781782420408.1.70

Shishoo, R. (2002). Recent developments in materials for use in protective clothing. International Journal of Clothing Science and Technology, 14(3–4), 201–215. https://doi.org/10.1108/09556220210437167

Song, G., Lu, Y., & Gholamreza, F. (2014). Clothing for protection against hot-liquid splash and steam hazards. Protective Clothing: Managing Thermal Stress, 90–111. https://doi.org/10.1533/9781782420408.1.90

Toma, D., Carpus, E., & Cohea, I. (2000). High visibility warning clothing. 1st European Conference on Protective Clothing, 88–93.

Wissler, E. H. (2014). Cold-exposure survival and modeling offshore antiexposure garments. In Protective Clothing: Managing Thermal Stress. Woodhead Publishing Limited. https://doi.org/10.1533/9781782420408.3.392

Index

Colour Plates

Fig.1.2 Shade Net

Fig.1.3 Bird Protection Net

Fig.1.4 Mulch Mat

(pg 4)

Fig.1.5 Awning

Fig.1.6 Architectural Membranes

Fig.1.7 Tarpaulins

(pg 6)

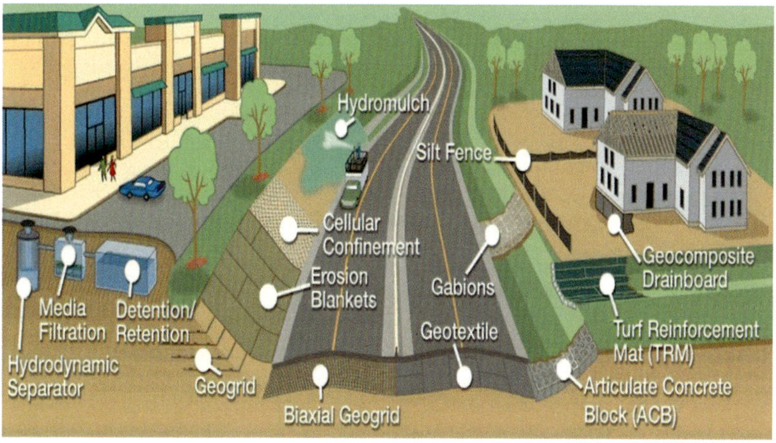

Fig.1.11

(pg 8)

Fig.1.8 Sewing Threads

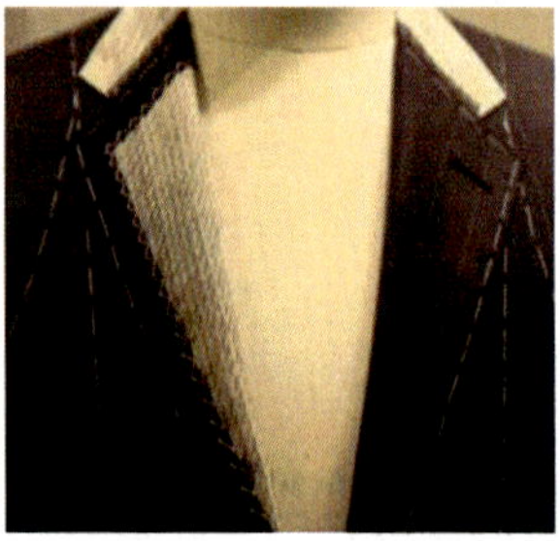

Fig.1.9 Interlining

Fig. 1.10 Shoe Laces

(pg 7)

Fig.1.12 Pillow

Fig.1.13 Carpet Backing

Fig.1.14 Fiberfill

(pg 9)

Fig.1.15 Conveyor Belts

Fig.1.16 Rope

Fig.1.17 Cigarette Filter Rods

(pg 11)

Fig.1.18 Convey

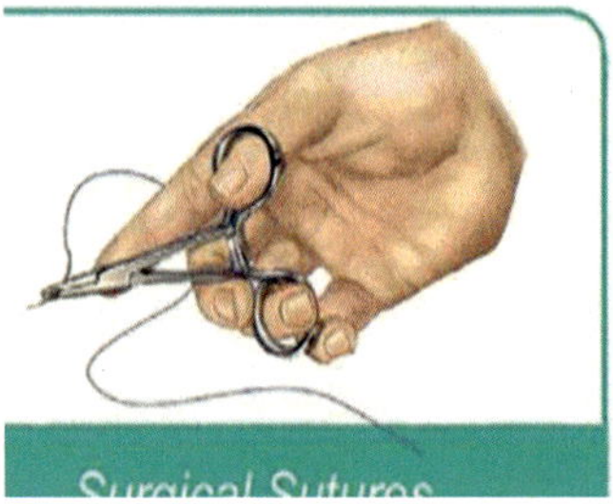

Fig.1.19 Surgical Sutures

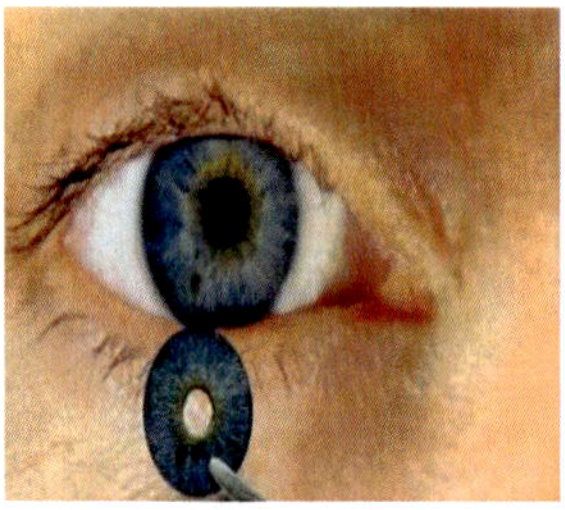

Fig.1.20 Artificial Implants

(pg 12)

Fig.1.21 Tyrecords

Fig.1.22 Air bags

Fig.1.23 Seat Covers

(pg 13)

Fig.1.24 Tyrecords

Fig.1.25 Tea Bags

Fig.1.26 Flexible Intermidiate Bulk Containers

(pg 15)

Fig.1.27 Fire Retardant Clothing

Fig.1.28 Bulletproof Jacket

Fig.1.29 High Altitude Clothing

(pg 17)

Fig.1.30 Parachute

Fig.1.31 Sleeping Bag

Fig.1.32 Astro turf

(pg 17)

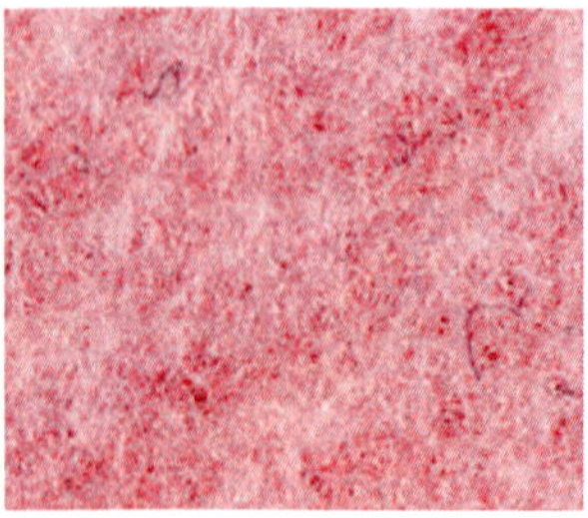

Fig.2.1 Woven Fabric

Fig.2.2 Knitted Fabric

Fig.2.3 Bonded Fabric

(pg 23)

Fig. 2.4 Endoskeletal prostheses

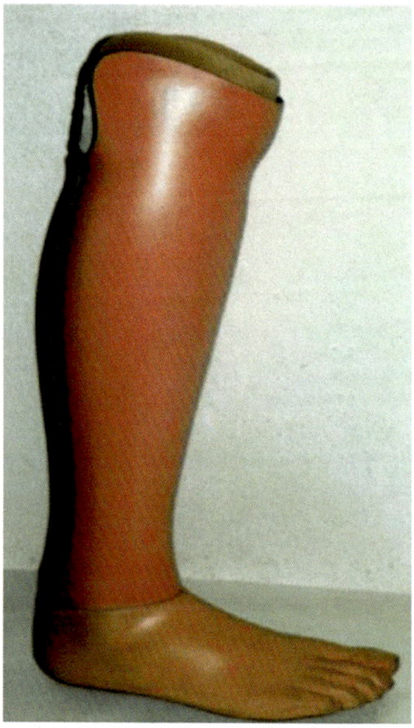

Fig. 2.5 Exoskeletal prostheses

(pg 26)

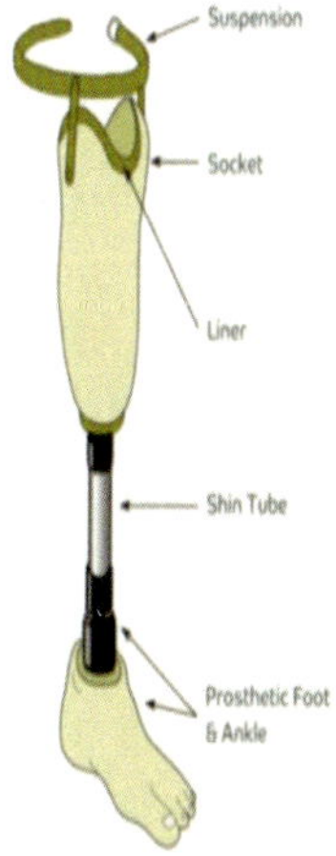

Fig.2.6 Components of Lower limb prostheses

(pg 26)

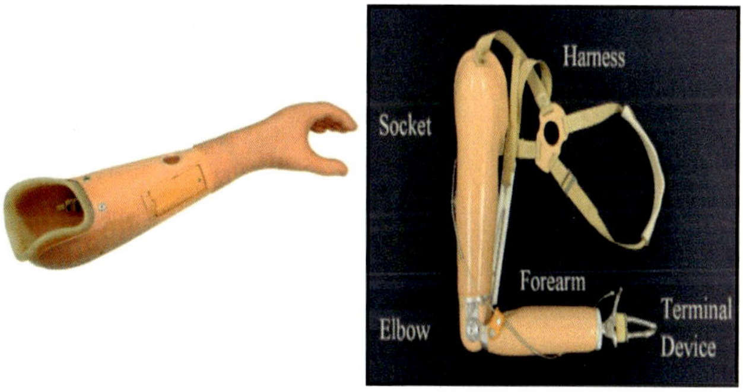

Fig. 2.7 Upper Limb Prostheses

(pg 27)

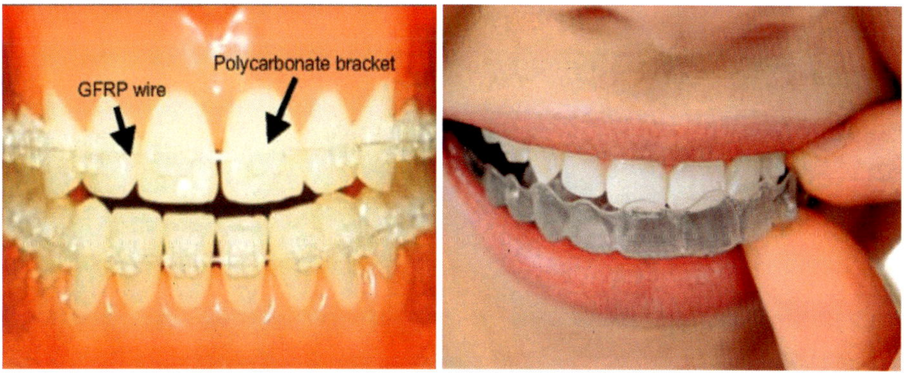

Fig.2.8 Orthodontics

(pg 29)

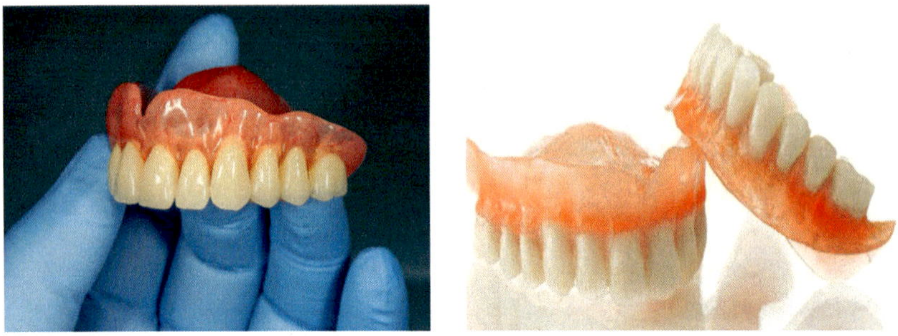

Fig. 2.9 Prosthodontics

(pg 30)

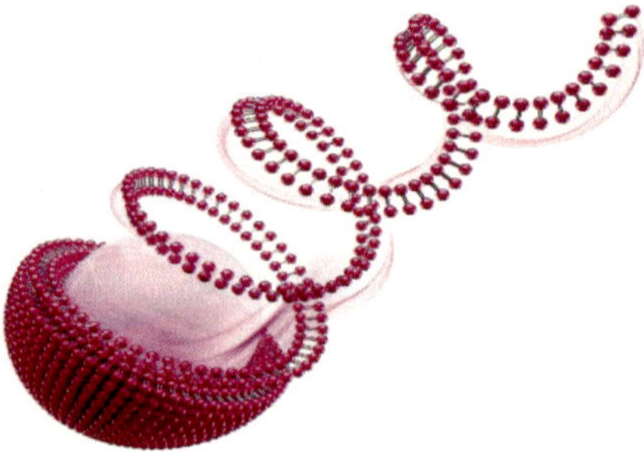

Fig 3.1: Microencapsulation structure

(pg 34)

Fig.4.1: Malani pattu shawl

(pg 45)

Fig. 4.2: A section of Malani pattu shawl

(pg 47)

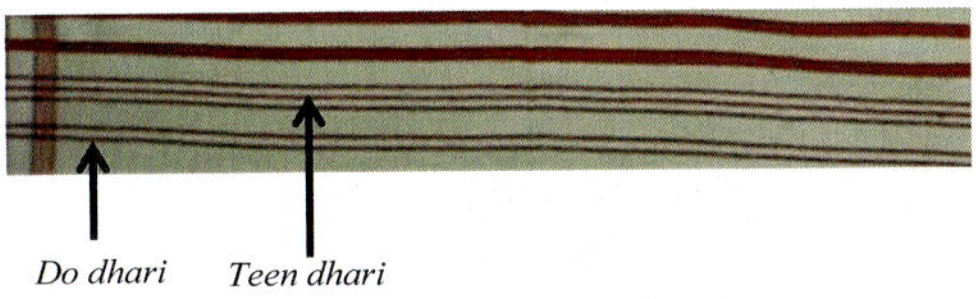

Fig. 4.3: A section of malani pattu

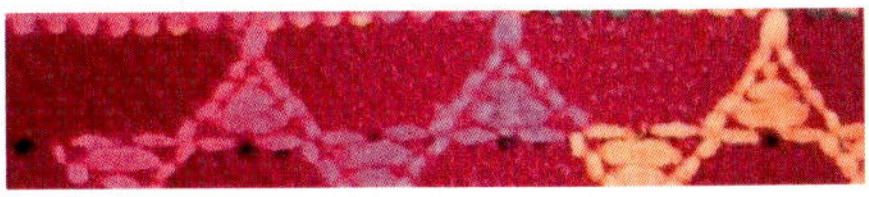

Figure 4.4: Sankli pattern

(pg 47)

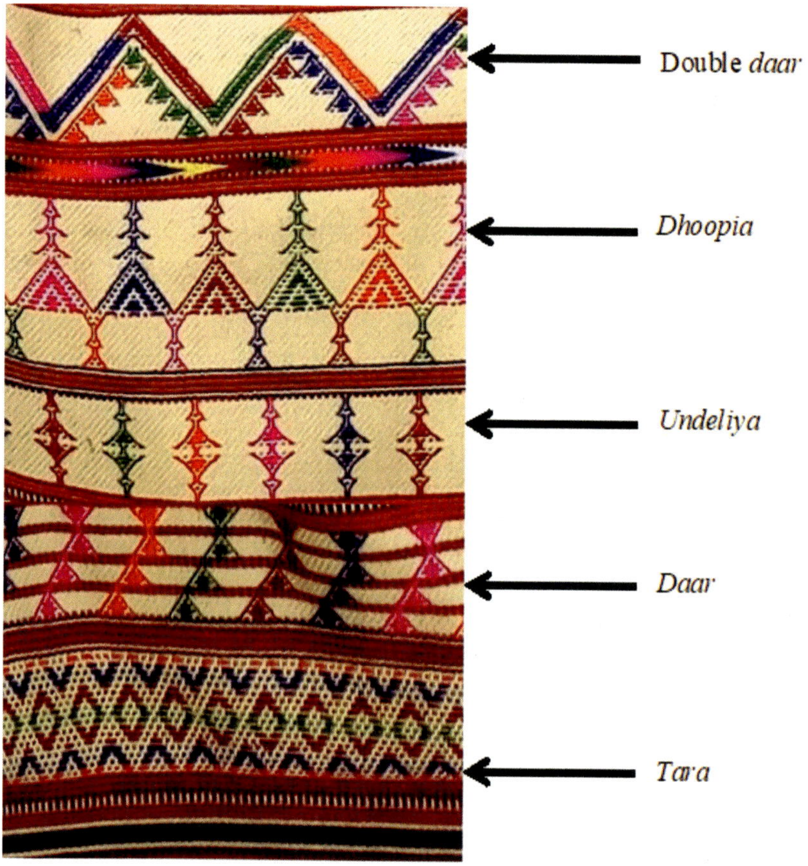

Figure 4.5: A section of Malani pattu shawl

(pg 48)

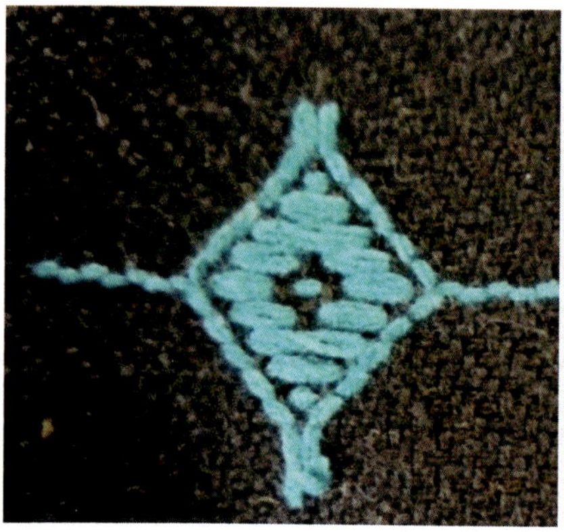

Fig. 4.6: Phool motif

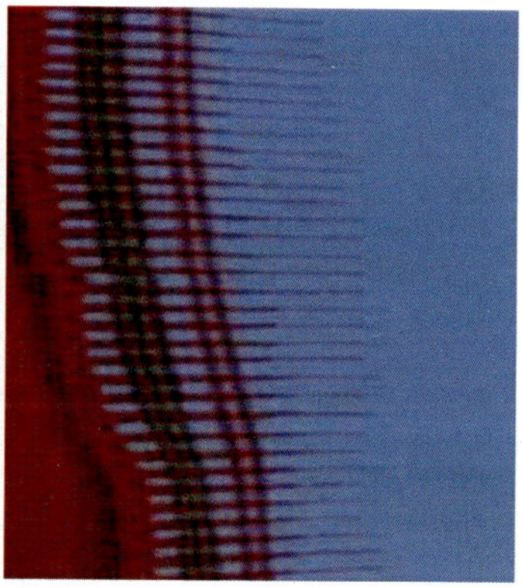

Fig. 4.7: Chotiya pattern

(pg 50)

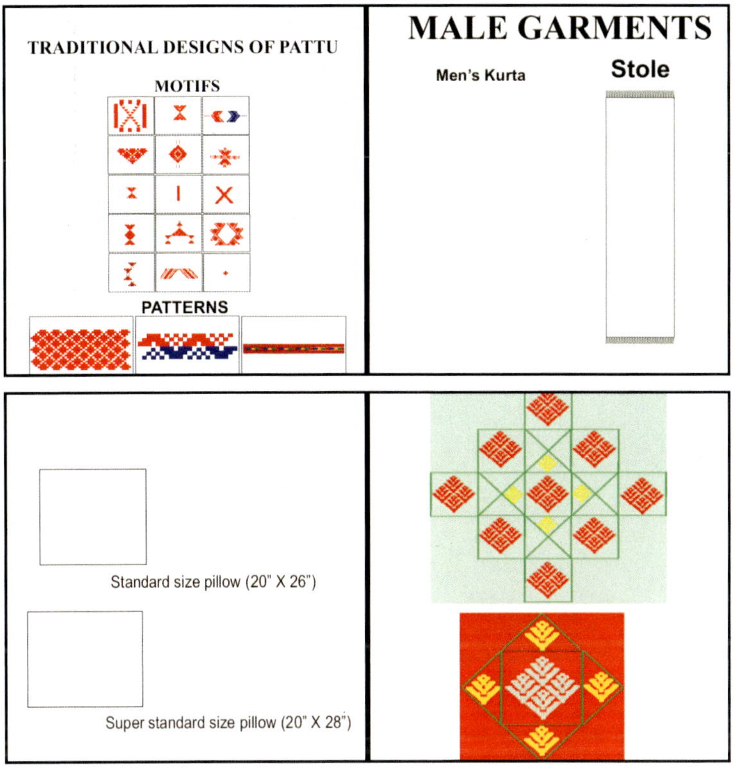

Fig. 4.8: Screenshots of Interactive CD

(pg 51)

Fig.5.1

(pg 54)

Fig. 5.2

(pg 55)

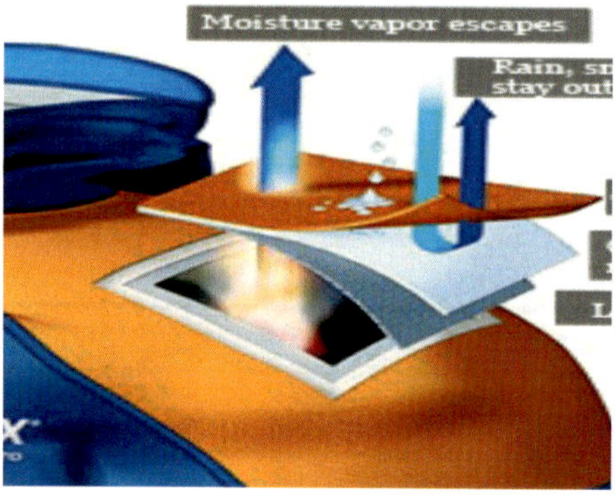

Fig. 6.2

(pg 65)

Fig. 6.1

(pg 64)

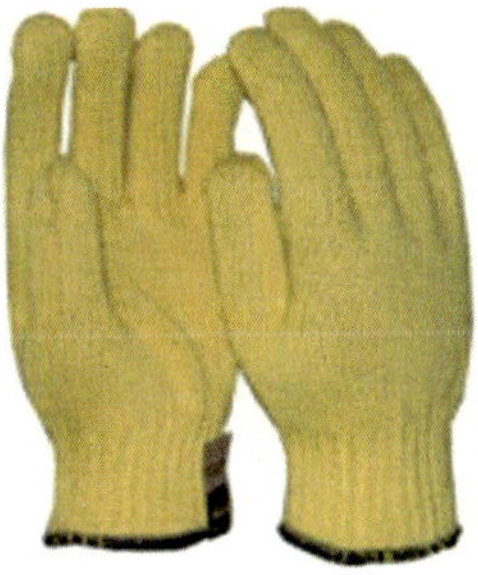

Fig. 6.4 Cut Resistant Gloves

Fig. 6.5 Chain Saw Clothing

Fig. 6.6 Puncture Resistant Gloves

(pg 67)

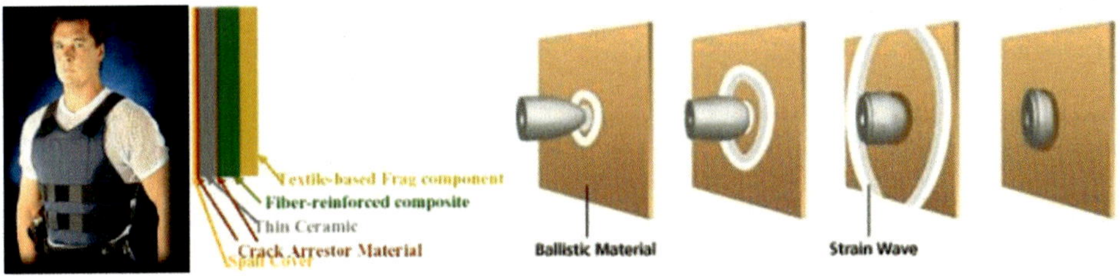

Fig. 6.7 Bullet Proof Vest Components

(pg 68)

Fig. 9.1: Sustainable Development Goals (SDGs)

(pg 92)

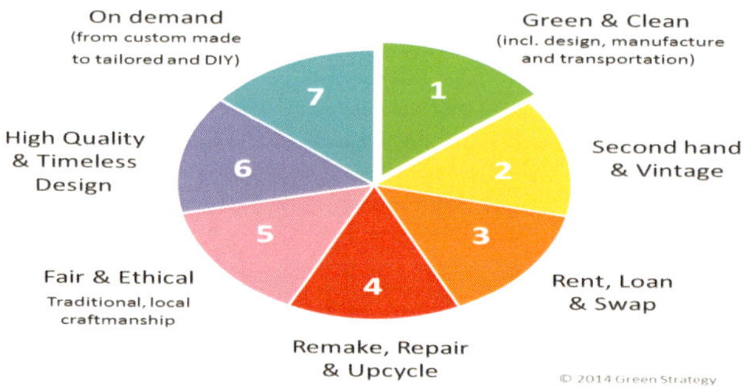

Fig.9.2: Seven forms of sustainable fashion

(pg 93)

Fig. 10.1

(pg 102)

Fig. 10.2 Ajrakh block printing

Fig. 10.3 Bagru block printing

(pg 104)

Fig.10.4 Sanganer block printing

Fig.10.5 Kalamkari block printing

(pg 105)

Fig.10.6 Natural dyed fibre

(pg 106)

Fig.10.7 Natural dyed yarn

(pg 106)

Fig.10.8 Dyed Fabric

(pg 107)

Fig.10.9 Dyed Garments

(pg 107)

Fig.10.10 Space dyeing

(pg 108)

Fig.10.11 Shibori

Fig.10.12 Roller

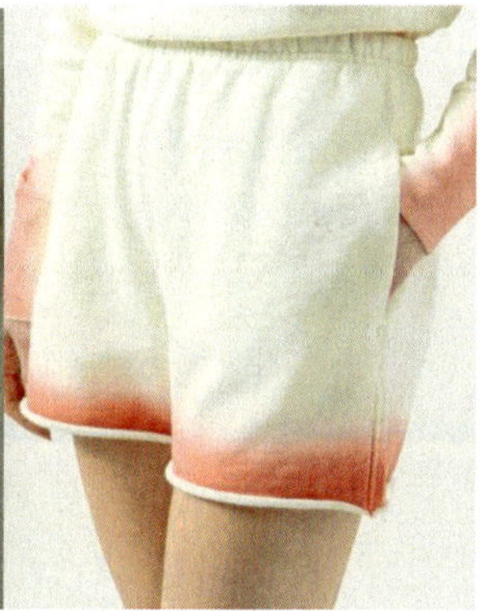

Fig.10.13 Spray

(pg 108)

Fig.10.14 Painted effect

Fig.10.15 Dry brush stroke

Fig.10.16 Spray effect

(pg 108)

Fig.12.1

(pg 124)

Fig. 12.2
(pg 126)

Fig. 12.3
(pg 126)

Fig. 12.4
(pg 127)

Fig. 12.5
(pg 128)

Fig 12.6
(pg 129)

Fig.12.7
(pg 130)

Fig. 12.8
(pg 131)

Fig. 12.9
(pg 132)

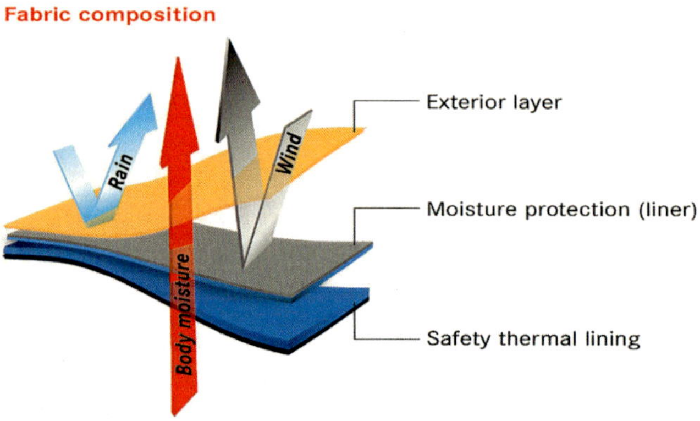

Fig.13.2 Fabric layer representation of rain and wind penetration
(pg 139)

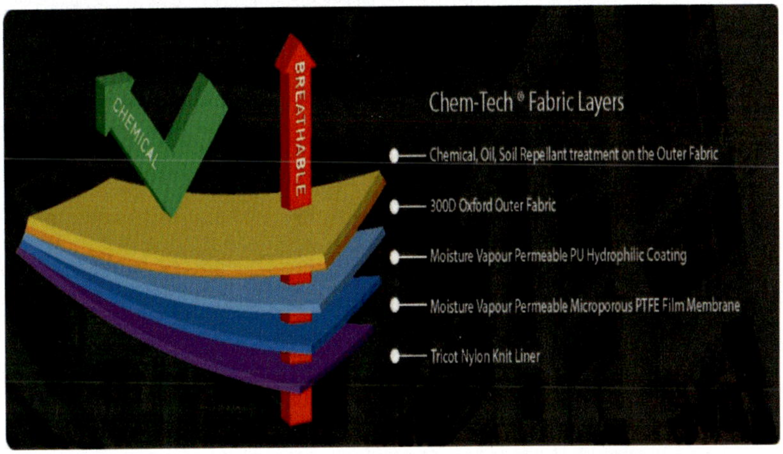

Fig.13.3 Fabric layer representation of chemical permeability

(pg 140)

Fig.13.5 Garments for visibility warning clothing

(pg 141)

Fig.13.6 Different parts of the military and ballistic protection clothing (pg 142)

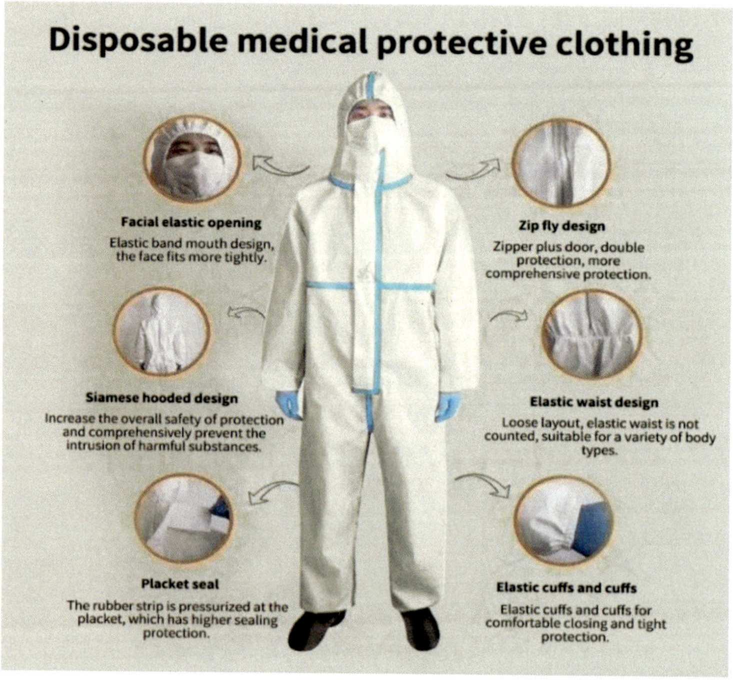

Fig.13.7 Personal protective equipment for medical protective clothing (pg 143)

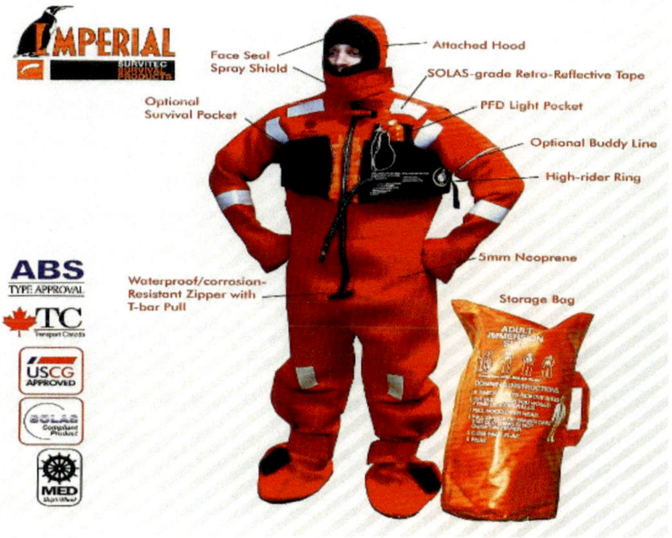

Fig.13.8 Survival suit for the underwater ejection

(pg 143)

Fig.13.9 Basic clothing items for multiple hazard protection

(pg 144)

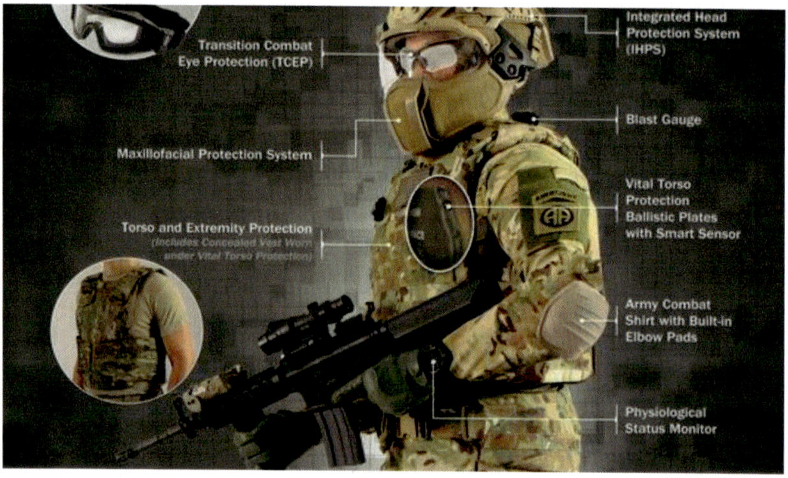

Fig.13.10 depicts the application of smart textiles in military

(pg 145)